# STRINGS

# HANDS

# SHADOWS

## A MODERN

# PUPPET

# HISTORY

**JOHN BELL**

THE DETROIT INSTITUTE OF ARTS

## COVER

This clown could juggle not only with his hands but also with his head. One string connects a ball to the juggler's head and another to his hand, which tosses the ball into the air before it bounces off his head. Made by American puppeteer Walter E. Deaves, the marionette dates to the late 19th or early 20th century.

## ACKNOWLEDGMENTS

The author wishes to thank Judith Ruskin, Larry Baranski, and Cathy Lauerman of the Detroit Institute of Arts for their enthusiastic support; Professor Salil Singh, Professor Kathy Foley, and Budi of Indonesia for their help in identifying Asian puppets; Rod Young for his advice; and Trudi Cohen for her continuing sustenance.

ISBN 0-89558-156-6

Library of Congress Cataloging-in-Publication Data is available.

Director, The Detroit Institute of Arts:
    Graham W. J. Beal
Director of Publications: Julia P. Henshaw
Director of Visual Resources: Dirk Bakker
DIAgram Series Editor: Judith A. Ruskin
Editorial Assistants: Tanya Pohrt, Kelli Carr
Design: Savitski Design, Ann Arbor, Michigan

Printed and bound in the United States of America.

The Detroit Institute of Arts is known for many outstanding works of art—Pieter Bruegel's *The Wedding Dance*, Diego Rivera's *Detroit Industry* murals, James McNeill Whistler's *Nocturne in Black and Gold: The Falling Rocket*, and a large African *Nail Figure*, to name just a few. Less well known, but certainly deserving of wider recognition, is the museum's extensive collection of puppets.

The Paul McPharlin Collection of Puppets and Theater Arts is one of the most significant groups of its kind in the country. At its core are the many puppets—hand puppets, marionettes, rod and shadow puppets—collected by Paul McPharlin (1903-48), a puppeteer, author, and designer with strong Michigan ties. His collection came to the Detroit Institute of Arts in 1951 as a gift from his parents and widow. It is through McPharlin's pioneering efforts to research the history of the art and preserve puppets and puppet theater that much information survives today.

*Strings, Hands, Shadows: A Modern Puppet History* examines the forces that have shaped today's puppet theater. Paul McPharlin took care to assemble examples from worldwide puppet traditions encompassing Europe, the Americas, and Asia. But his influence, particularly on modern American puppet theater, goes far beyond his extensive collection. As an active participant in the puppet revival of the early twentieth century, he and his fellow puppeteers laid the groundwork for the reinvention of puppet theater as a distinctive art form. The fruits of McPharlin's decidedly modernist views are evident in present-day puppet festivals and performances.

Author John Bell, using examples from the museum's eight hundred puppets and more than seven hundred related backdrops and props, traces the changing role of puppetry over the course of three centuries: from religious ritual to vaudeville-style entertainment; from serious theater to primarily children's programs; and to its recent reemergence as an adult theatrical form. Along with these transitions, he examines the cross-cultural influences of Asian, European, North and South American, and African puppet traditions on each other.

*Strings, Hands, Shadows: A Modern Puppet History* is the second volume in the Detroit Institute of Arts' new DIAgram book series. DIAgram books provide new ways of looking at the museum's permanent collection—both the familiar and the less so. The first of the series, *European Vistas/Cultural Landscapes*, offered an array of interpretations of the city and countryside viewed through the lens of many of our European masterpieces. In this book on puppets, the spotlight is turned on a less well known aspect of our collection, but one that certainly repays close examination.

The publication of this title would not have been possible without the hard work and dedication of numerous people. First and foremost is Larry Baranski, curator of the Paul McPharlin Puppetry Collection as well as an associate curator in the department of film. He consulted on all aspects of the publication and acted as "puppet wrangler" to get the puppets to the photography studio, where Dirk Bakker, director of visual resources, captured them on film as only he can. Judith Ruskin, as DIAgram editor, shepherded the manuscript and illustrations from their earliest stages into this book, with the assistance of editorial assistant Kelli Carr. Savitski Design of Ann Arbor, Michigan, produced the lively layout of the book. And of course, our thanks go to author John Bell, assistant professor of theater arts at Emerson College, Boston, who wrote the engaging text.

Graham W. J. Beal
*Director, Detroit Institute of Arts*

This complete Punch and Judy set shows the rough, colorful qualities of these popular puppet characters. Punch and Judy puppet shows originated in England, but this set of hand puppets was made in the United States in the mid-1800s. Pictured, from left to right, are Punch, Judy, Crocodile with Punch's Baby nestled in its mouth, Devil, Ghost, and Joey the Clown.

**P**aul McPharlin used this self-portrait puppet to introduce the shows for his Marionette Fellowship of Detroit troupe, which he founded in 1929. Puppeteers, like other artists, often made self-portraits. These likenesses frequently served as the puppeteer's alter ego.

Puppetry—the telling of stories in theatrical or ritual events combining humans and pieces of the surrounding physical world—is arguably the most widespread form of performance. Puppets can be traced as far back as ancient Egypt, Greece, and Rome and are found today in cultures worldwide, across the Americas, Europe, Africa, and Asia. The task of making this ancient art of puppetry work in the modern era is an ongoing endeavor. In the twentieth century puppeteers sought to expand  the role of puppet theater in modern society in many different directions: as a means of making popular entertainment, as art theater, as an educational tool, and as a means of persuasion. At different times and places puppeteers pursued various combinations of these goals, making "serious" drama, children's theater, promotional shows, commercials, political spectacle, films, and television shows. ◆ At the turn of the twenty-first century, a renaissance of puppet theater appears to be underway. In the United States during the 1990s, a theatrical production of Disney's *The Lion King* showed that a mask and puppet spectacle could become a runaway hit on Broadway, and the Jim Henson Foundation's series of bi-annual International

An INTRODUCTION to

1

Puppetry

Festivals of Puppet Theater began to expose new audiences to the richness and variety of innovative theater based on puppetry. Generations of children had grown up watching and learning from Jim Henson's Muppets on television, and a new appreciation of puppetry as a theater capable of conveying profound artistic, social, and political ideas, stories, and emotions had developed from the influence of Peter Schumann's

**N**ew York puppeteer Tony Sarg is credited with creating the first over-life-size inflatable figures used in parades. In this 1920s photograph, he is shown working in his studio on a large puppet for one of the first Thanksgiving Day parades organized by Macy's department store in New York City.

Bread and Puppet Theater, which had begun in the 1960s.

But the appearance of a puppet renaissance is somewhat deceptive, for puppetry is an art that sees fit to renew itself continually, as new generations of performers, sculptors, painters, writers, and audiences discover the possibilities of playing with material objects in performance. There is an uncanny similarity, in fact, between sentiments expressed in the 1920s and the current sense of a puppet revival. In 1926 puppeteer Remo Bufano, flush from the success of his own triumphs with puppet theater on Broadway, predicted a "renaissance of the marionette" in American theater. In fact, Bufano's prediction was quite correct, and the 1920s puppet renaissance was the first in a series of modern discoveries of the possibilities of

puppet theater. Our sense of the nature of those first modern puppet renaissances is valuable for our sense of the current one.

A fine record of this perpetual rebirth is the puppet collection at the Detroit Institute of Arts, based largely on the accumulation of puppets and related materials put together by Paul McPharlin during the years in which he was a major participant in the first puppet revival. The museum's collection has continued to grow as further elements were added during the more than fifty years since McPharlin's death. The collection lays out clearly and in rich detail the complex paths followed by puppeteers in the twentieth century as they redefined traditional forms from Europe and around the globe in order to reflect the changes brought about by the modern world.

McPharlin was more than an interested observer of the puppet phenomenon—in fact, he was a major player in its development and in the first half of the twentieth century perhaps the most important single force in establishing puppet theater's legitimacy and continuing presence in American culture. Like many puppeteers, he was a multi-talented individual: not only a performer, but a designer and builder as well. He was also a writer, editor, historian, curator, and organizer. From the moment he discovered puppets as a college student at Columbia University, to his untimely death from brain cancer in 1948

**P**aul McPharlin had a multifaceted career, as a writer, book designer, interior and theater-set designer, illustrator, and teacher, but it is for puppetry that he is best known. He was born on December 22, 1903, to William and Frances McPharlin in Detroit. His father's job necessitated frequent moves, and before graduating from high school in 1920, McPharlin lived in Toledo, Ohio, Washington D.C., New York City, and in between, Detroit.

After one year at a junior college in Detroit, McPharlin enrolled in New York's Columbia University. There he edited the student literary magazine, served as art director for the student yearbook, and designed sets and costumes for theatrical productions. After he assisted a faculty member in the production of a rod puppet show, McPharlin found his niche.

After his 1924 graduation, McPharlin visited Europe and North Africa. Upon his return, he joined his parents, now in Chicago, where he wrote extensively and worked as an interior and graphic designer. Among his projects was the complete design of a candy store, from the overhead light fixtures to the wrappers for the sweets. At the same time, he and a partner organized a theater for classical drama. When it provided only limited financial success, McPharlin changed his focus to puppetry. In 1928 he founded the Marionette Fellowship of Evanston, Illinois, where he continued to produce dramatic theater at a fraction of the cost of live theater. With the onset of the Depression, he lost his designing job and left Chicago.

**P**aul McPharlin is shown here with Punch and Judy hand puppets from his 1931 show *Punch's Circus*.

McPharlin returned to Detroit, where he dedicated himself to puppetry and publishing. In 1929 he founded the Marionette Fellowship of Detroit and published his first book, *A Repertory of Marionette Plays*. At the invitation of the Detroit Institute of Arts, he presented a series of marionette plays in 1930. He planned the 1933 World's Fair National Exhibit of Puppets in Chicago. In 1936 he organized the first American Puppetry Conference and Festival, an event held in Detroit, which led to the founding of the Puppeteers of America a year later. McPharlin served as the group's first president.

Throughout the 1930s he designed and published over fifty books and pamphlets on the art of puppetry. Starting in 1930 he edited and published *Puppetry: An International Yearbook of Puppets and Marionettes*, chronicling the experiences of puppeteers around the globe. Also in the 1930s, he taught art

and puppetry courses at a variety of Detroit-area locations including Wayne University (now Wayne State University), where he received a Master of Arts degree in 1938. He was director of the Detroit Artisan Guild, which produced both puppet and live theater plays. With the completion of his dissertation "Puppets in American Life: 1524–1918," he earned a Ph.D. from the University of Michigan. In 1941 he was made supervisor of the Michigan Arts and Craft Project, a division of the federal Work Projects Administration.

McPharlin was drafted into the army in 1942 and sent to Keesler Field in Mississippi, where he was trained as an air mechanic. However, he also worked as an illustrator and librarian and performed puppet shows with his marionette Rookie Joe to demonstrate military safety rules. When the army put him on inactive duty in 1943, McPharlin returned to Detroit to work for a short time designing catalogues and drawing illustrations of machine-engine parts. In 1944 he went to New York, where he worked as an illustrator, typographer, book designer, and interior designer. In 1948 he married his long-time friend and fellow puppeteer, Marjorie Batchelder. Shortly thereafter, McPharlin was diagnosed with a malignant brain tumor. He died on September 28, 1948, at the home of his parents in Birmingham, Michigan.

Paul McPharlin's collection of puppets, along with related items and an extensive library containing many rare books on puppet history and theater, was given to the Detroit Institute of Arts in 1951 by his parents, Mr. and Mrs. William H. J. McPharlin, and his widow, Marjorie Batchelder McPharlin.

## TYPES OF PUPPETS AND OBJECT THEATER

**Hand puppets** are diminutive figures that the puppeteer operates with fingers and wrist from within the puppet's glove-like structure, thus becoming extensions of the puppeteer's hands.

Japanese-style **Bunraku puppets** are full-figured half- or three-quarter-size human figures operated by two or three puppeteers who directly control the puppet in full view of the audience.

**Rod puppets** extend the distance between operator and object by means of the control rods used to manipulate them, but the rods maintain the direct movement relationship between operator and puppet characteristic of hand puppets.

**Marionettes** are flexible, full-figure representations of humans and animals operated by strings (although some use a combination of rods and strings). Manipulation is a bit indirect because the marionette's strings do not respond with the immediacy of rod and hand puppets. Nonetheless, marionettes are often capable of finer and more delicate movements.

**Over-life-size puppets** change the ratio between performer and puppet. Sometimes the puppeteer will be fully enclosed inside such figures, as in the walk-around puppets used in theme parks and sporting events, or the abstract puppets designed by Joan Miró for the play *Mori el Merma*. Other over-size puppets, such as the inflatables invented by Tony Sarg for Macy's Thanksgiving Day parades in New York, or the float designed by Remo Bufano for a wartime patriotic parade in the same city, require a number of operators to manipulate them.

**Shadow puppets** are generally flat rod puppets whose shadow (black or in translucent colors) is projected against a cloth screen by a light source mounted behind the puppets. Such puppets present an intriguing means of performance, since the audience does not watch the puppet itself, but its shadow image, a method that also suggests the more technologically advanced performance forms of film, television, and computer imaging, also based on images projected onto screens.

The Detroit Institute of Arts collections also include other forms of object theater outside the realm of puppets. Among them are a variety of masks from African, Asian, European, and American traditions. These objects, even more than hand puppets, are operated directly by the performer's body, almost like a second skin. A mask would be only one part of the attire needed to transform the wearer into another being or spirit. In a masquerade of the Dan culture in Africa's Ivory Coast, for example a performer would add a cape and short fiber skirt to a dance mask (above) to complete his transformation. In addition, the museum has a number of examples of picture performance, in which the center of attention is not a human or animal effigy, but a two-dimensional picture explained by a narrator, who points out and elaborates upon the images contained in it.

**Hand Puppet**

**Bunraku Puppet**

**Rod Puppet**

at the age of forty-four, McPharlin was a tireless proselytizer for the cultural importance of puppet theater, not only as a viable means of making contemporary theater but as a world-wide cultural treasure. Together with Marjorie Batchelder, another puppet enthusiast who was his long-time friend and colleague, and whom he married the year before his death, McPharlin articulated his vision of the modern importance of puppet theater. He published books and articles; organized exhibits, conferences, and festivals; helped found the Puppeteers of America; and above all built and performed puppet shows of remarkable artistic integrity and beauty.

McPharlin's collection, and the pieces added later, stand as one of the United States's important physical records of the development of puppetry worldwide. But perhaps even more than that, the collection stands as a remarkable testament to the ingenuity and inspired skill

hundreds of people applied to the task of making beautiful, comic, serious, and mostly humble theater out of wood, paper, cloth, metal, and plastic, as well as their own bodies and voices. That work, often by little-known or anonymous women and men, can still inspire us, as it so obviously inspired McPharlin and Batchelder.

## PUPPETS AND PERFORMING OBJECTS

The various types of puppets and other objects that have traditionally been used in performance all fall under the definition of what anthropologist Frank Proschan calls "performing objects": "material images of humans, animals, or spirits that are created, displayed, or manipulated in narrative or dramatic performance." Proschan's term is intriguing because it obviously includes objects (such as masks or pictures used in performance) that are not, strictly

speaking, puppets; it also could include such modern means of communication as film, television, and computers, connections that offer all sorts of food for thought.

A good means of conceptualizing the different forms of puppet and object theater is to consider the distance of the object from the puppeteer and the means of manipulation consequent to that distance. But in all of the many forms of puppet and object performance, a consistent principle applies: the center of attention, for both performers and audience, is the material object—the puppet. We choose to believe that this combination of wood, clay, cloth, metal, or plastic is capable of telling us something about ourselves and others. The main difference, then, between puppet theater and actors' theater is the confidence that a material image, not simply a human being alone, can recount a story to its audience. ◆

**Marionette**

**Over-Life-Size Puppet**

**Shadow Puppet**

These three Venetian hand puppets are typical of those used by itinerant puppeteers who traveled throughout Italy performing the social satire of *commedia dell'arte*. The finery of the lovers (two puppets at left) stands in contrast to the more rugged features of Capitano, the braggart soldier (at right). The elaborate stage surrounding the puppets is the original 18th-century one on which these figures were first performed.

Two of the more notable aspects of puppet theater are its everyday commonness, and—especially in the West—its typical exclusion from the ranks of high culture. This has made its European history somewhat murky, although puppet historians have been able to trace its broad developments over the centuries. In the earliest periods of European history, puppets and objects functioned as they have in other parts of the world, as central elements of community rituals and religious performances, as well as everyday purveyors of entertainment and social satire. Puppets and automata (mechanically operated figures like the steampowered statues of gods designed by noted inventor Hero of Alexandria) figured prominently in Greek and Roman religious and secular culture. But puppets, masks, and sacred or semi-sacred performing objects were also central to the lives of tribal, village, and later urban life in every community on the continent. ◆ Puppet history can be traced, some six centuries later, to medieval animated altarpiece figures first found in churches. These figures were succeeded by hand puppets, which

2

EUROPEAN PUPPETS

*in the*

**W**Old & New**ORLDS**

were then joined by marionettes, as traveling companies ranged across Europe, intermixing styles and stories, and permanent theaters rose, fell, and reappeared in the growing cities. The growth of the middle class in the eighteenth century inspired a new range of puppet theaters focused on that audience, and in the early nineteenth century the Romantic writers and philosophers of that era seized upon puppet theater as somehow rough and true, an antidote to the purported rationality of modern and increasingly industrialized life. By the end of the nineteenth century, puppetry seemed poised to enter the next as a recognized "modern" art form.

This fancily dressed gentleman is representative of a strong 18th-century Italian marionette tradition. He is from a set of marionettes, possibly from Venice. The puppets may have been used to perform the tragedy of Dr. Faust, one of the most popular plays in Europe.

## EUROPEAN PUPPET TRADITIONS

By the eighteenth century, hand puppet and marionette theater were established popular entertainment forms, although they were not generally considered to be "high" culture (a situation that persists to this day). Traveling performers, especially from Italy, had for two centuries wandered throughout all of Europe, performing the improvised social satire of *commedia dell'arte*—sometimes with leather half-masks and other times with puppets. Such performances would influence all levels of dramatic tradition, from Shakespeare and Molière to Russian street performers. A set of Venetian hand puppets demonstrates the structure of such *commedia* shows. Typically, two elegant young lovers face the opposition of one or more parents. Comic masked characters (usually servants) are wholly involved in complicated, often outlandish, but always hilarious strategies to get the lovers together, an enterprise that invariably succeeds by the end of the show.

A related and equally strong tradition is reflected in eighteenth-century Italian marionettes, which in the museum's collection include a fancy couple, a red horned devil with metal wings, and a rougher, mustachioed figure who might be a robber. These marionettes, possibly from Venice, could have been used to perform the tragedy of Dr. Faust, whose tale of selling his soul to the devil was one of the most popular plays in the European puppet repertoire. The puppets' clear-cut and instantly recognizable distinctions between good and evil, nobles and commoners, tell a good deal about important issues in eighteenth-century Europe and how puppet theater directly dealt with them. Unlike later multistringed marionettes, these puppets show a simple control system: just one metal rod attached to a ring in the head, and one string that is connected to both hands. With such straightforward controls, the skill of the puppeteer lies in understanding how the movement of puppet parts under his or her command will affect the more subtle movement of those extremities indirectly connected to those parts.

The marionettes of Pietro Radillo, a century later, show how European marionette controls became more complex, a development that some historians connect to the late nineteenth century's increasing fascination with realism (see p. 16, top). Instead of a rod and two strings, Radillo's marionettes are controlled by up to eight separate strings, which offer the possibility of more direct control of each body part.

Also during the nineteenth century, a somewhat different Italian marionette tradition emerged to the south, in Sicily (see p. 16, bottom). The *opera dei pupi* was

"Marionettes touch…on everything in the world which is most grave and consequential; on sciences, on fine arts, on poetry, on religious ceremonies, on politics. Enchanting little creatures… marionettes have received from sculpture, form; from painting, color; from mechanics, movement; from poetry, words; from music, song; from the dance, grace and the measure of steps and gesture; and finally from improvisation, the most precious of privileges, liberty of free speech."

Charles Magnin, *Histoire des Marionnettes en Europe*, 1862

These two elegantly dressed Venetian gentleman (left), made by Pietro Radillo in the late 19th century, may have been used in puppet versions of popular Italian operas or romantic dramas.

The man, woman, priest and knight in armor are 19th-century Sicilian rod marionettes, operated from above by a combination of strings and metal rods. Such puppets performed in epic tales of love, honor, betrayal, and knightly battles, often centering around the exploits of the knight Orlando. These stories collectively became known as *Orlando Furioso*, taking the name from the central character. The puppets are quite heavy, weighing close to forty pounds each.

an exceedingly popular form of entertainment. It drew on chivalrous French medieval epics to tell the stories of Christian knights, led by the Emperor Charlemagne, against the Muslim Saracens. The material paralleled the subject matter of many epic Asian puppet forms. In nightly episodes—sometimes as many as four hundred in a row—Sicilian puppeteers would present the ongoing dramas of love, honor, betrayal and (always!) battle that marked the life of the knight Orlando, his love Angelica, their king Charlemagne, and their nemesis, the treacherous knight Gano de Maganza.

At least since the time of *commedia dell'arte*, European puppet theater has been involved in a complex symbiotic relationship with actors' theater, whose character types and repertoire regularly turn up, in truncated and sometimes broader form, on the puppet stage. This was true for serious dramas, but also for comedy and variety shows, especially in the nineteenth century. Variety shows, which eschewed dramatic plot for a succession of entertaining separate acts, were enormously popular across Europe, especially as performed by English marionette troupes. Taking stock characters from English pantomime shows (which were in turn inspired by the *commedia* tradition) and American minstrel shows, variety puppet shows were a flexible, often stunning way to attract and hold an audience, especially in combination with puppet versions of popular melodramas.

The assortment of possibilities offered by this form is large. In the museum collection alone there are dancing girls, a colorful dancing sailor, a milkmaid, two fencers, and such comic figures as a policeman, nurse, and witch. But the most spectacular puppets stunned nineteenth-century audiences with their spectacular tricks, or sudden on-stage transformations from one character into one or more others. For example, an acrobat puppet juggled not only with his hands but also with his head; another acrobat walked a tightrope; a clown could stretch its neck to twice the height of its body; and a "Grand Turk" trick marionette, an exotic character figuratively representing the Ottoman Empire (see pp. 17-18). Some of these feats imitated contemporary circus, pantomime, and variety-show acts, but others—especially the transformations—could only be accomplished on the puppet stage, something enterprising puppeteers made full use of as English marionette companies—and their French and American imitators—toured the world.

While 19th-century puppet theater often imitated contemporary circus and variety show acts, some feats, particularly transformations and tricks, could only be performed on the puppet stage. The neck of this trick marionette, the Grand Turk, can extend another eight inches.

A particularly interesting marker of the cultural importance of European puppets is the emergence of regional or national heroes in every European country as marionettes or hand puppets. Characters such as Punch (derived from the *commedia* character Pulcinello), Guignol, Kasperl, and Petrushka represented, respectively, English, French, German, and Russian character traits. This is not to say that such characters symbolized particularly admirable or patriotic traits; instead they tended to represent the scrappy, bawdy, anti-authoritarian, and even anarchistic impulses that appealed to working-class audiences in the newly burgeoning urban communities of Europe. As a consequence, the theaters of Punch, Kasperl, Guignol, Petrushka and other

regional favorites were kept under close scrutiny by the authorities, who censored shows featuring sexually or politically suspect material. Puppet historians have pointed out that the best place to glean information about these puppet theaters is in police records.

European puppet troupes in the nineteenth century were often family enterprises that passed on the crafts of building puppets and inventing shows from one generation to the next. Some puppeteers took advantage of the rapidly growing cities of the era by setting up permanent puppet theaters to attract a regular stream of working-class and middle-class audiences, comprising both adults and children. But also, in a practical tradition stemming back to the *commedia* troupes of the Renaissance, other

European puppet companies spent all of their time on the road, traveling from town to town on a well-worn route, often in horse-drawn wagons.

George William Middleton, an English puppeteer whose family "worked with marionettes" for generations, described the nineteenth-century repertoire of the Middleton Brothers Marionettes as combining popular melodramas with variety show numbers and transformations in a very full evening's entertainment:

> We used both three-foot and fourteen-inch marionettes, depending on the hall in which we played. Our performances…generally opened with a Negro minstrel first part, with nine characters; then came from twelve to fifteen olio specialties, including eight quadrille dancers and fairies. Then came a drama,

The assortment of possible acts for
puppet variety shows acts was
enormous. These three marionettes—
juggler, tight rope walker, and clown—
are clearly based on circus performances.
English marionette troupes toured the
world during the 19th century, and their
influence was felt in France and the
United States as companies imitated
the variety-show format.

chosen from our repertory of *The Miller and His Men, Othello, Beauty and the Beast, Colleen Bawn, The Sea of Ice, The Vampire's Bride, Babes in the Wood, Little Red Riding Hood, Cinderella, The Seven Clerks, Poll and Her Partner Joe, Robin Rough Head, Dick Whittington and His Cat, Jack and the Beanstalk, Jack the Giant Killer, As You Like It,* and many others. Each drama was in three, four, or five scenes, and took about fifteen people to work; the backcloths were dropped one over the other for quick changes. After the play there followed fifteen or twenty pantomime tricks, and the performance closed with a grand transformation scene.

Like the Middleton family in England, France's Dulaar-Roussel family troupe, the Théâtre des Lilliputiens, traveled throughout that country with an array of different puppet theater forms. Founded in 1895 by Louis Roussel and his wife Victorine Levergeois, the troupe performed exclusively at French village fairs. Their repertoire included such classic marionette pieces as *The Temptation of Saint Anthony, Puss 'n Boots,* and *Little Red Riding Hood,* as well as variety shows featuring flat cut-out metal transformation puppets which could, for example, metamorphose from a man riding a donkey to a donkey riding a man. The Dulaar-Roussel troupe also featured shadow theater and hand-puppet shows.

## EUROPEAN TRADITIONS IN THE NEW WORLD

Upon their arrival in the New World, Europeans encountered a variety of thriving puppet forms in the different native cultures. But, beginning with the two puppeteers (Pedro López and Manuel Rodríquez) who happened to accompany the Spanish conquistador Hernando Cortez on his first trip to Mexico in 1519, Europeans brought their own puppet traditions with them. In his *Puppet Theatre in America*, Paul McPharlin traced the first performances of English-language puppet theater to the early eighteenth century in New York. Undoubtedly, those performances duplicated popular European forms, but over the next two centuries puppets in America gradually developed their own particular styles and characters.

German, Italian, Irish, Greek, and English immigrants all brought with them aspects of their respective puppet traditions, and the English Punch and Judy in particular developed into a fixture of nine-teenth-century American puppet theater. Eminently portable and easy to stage—in a park, on a street corner, on a beach, on stage as part of a variety show, or on the midway of a traveling circus—this vibrant, hilarious, and also darkly disturbing show attracted audiences of all kinds and ages. Although modified by each Punch performer,

These hand puppets (opposite) were part of shows performed by the Dulaar-Roussel family troupe, the Théâtre des Lilliputiens, at French village fairs. The two puppets at the upper left are the scrappy Guignol, the French national hero who exhibited many of the same character traits as the English Punch. The other puppets in this set include a policeman (upper right), two women (lower left and center), and a wide-eyed man (lower right).

and subject to the improvisatory impulses of each separate performance, the basic story remains the same: the big-nosed, hump-backed Punch, whose voice is a reedy whistle produced by a "swazzle" (a small vibrating reed lodged in the puppeteer's mouth), accidentally kills his baby, and then (with a certain glee) similarly eliminates his entire community: his wife, the Doctor, the Judge, Policeman, Jack Ketch the Hangman, and any other characters a puppeteer might want to add in. The threat of just retribution occurs in a series of appearances by Ghosts, the Devil, and a man-eating Crocodile, and the ending of the show heads toward a finale of sin punished, recalling the moral certainties of medieval European theater. Yet either implicitly or explicitly, Punch manages to get away with his transgressions: he cheats the Hangman and tricks the Devil; and the Crocodile who devours him admits, in a venerable line, that he "might let him out for the very next show." In other words, Punch gets away with it all. The Punch and Judy hand puppets feature boldly sculpted design and are brightly painted, qualities that clearly made them "read" well from a distance.

A set of Punch and Judy hand puppets (left) from the late nineteenth century belonged to George "Punch" Irving, a New Hampshire native who worked with traveling circuses and sideshows before becoming a puppeteer. The Irving puppets also reveal an important aspect of nineteenth-century American theater: its attention to the various ethnic groups that were coming to define the nature of United States society. In addition to the representatives of family, religious, and social orders of the English tradition, Irving's puppets include a "Chinaman" and "Sambo," a black character, which reflect the particularly American consciousness of—and anxiety about—race, class, and ethnicity.

Puppet theater has traditionally existed in a close symbiotic relationship with other forms of theater, and this was particularly true of western performance in the nineteenth century. Actors' theater in nineteenth-century Europe and North America did not produce a wealth of brilliantly written dramas, but it did create great and entertaining visual spectacle. The nineteenth-century stage reveled in transformations and technical dexterity, presenting a variety of new performance methods, from toy theater to the moving panorama, which presaged the appearance of later spectacular inventions—especially film and television—in the following century.

Nineteenth-century melodramas were famous for their visual splendor: a river strewn with ice floes

hen
Punch first appeared in
17th-century English puppet
shows, his wife was named Joan.
The name was changed to Judy
because it was easier to pronounce
when speaking through a swazzle,
a device that gave the puppeteer's
voice a buzzing, metallic tone.

A complete set of 19th-century American Punch and Judy hand puppets (opposite), made by George "Punch" Irving, includes not only all of the standard characters but essential stage props, such as Punch's cudgel, the Hangman's gallows, and a coffin, as well. The puppets show signs of extensive use: both Punch's and Judy's noses have almost disappeared, victims of the innumerable beatings they experienced in performance.

One of the strengths of the McPharlin Puppetry Collection is the more than thirty examples from Daniel Meader's Royal Marionettes. A 19th-century American puppeteer, Meader followed the established European variety show format in his productions, presenting a series of unrelated acts. These included Punch and Judy shows, transformation puppets, and minstrel acts. Punch and the two devils shown here are from the same set of Punch and Judy marionettes.

Transformation puppets were often designed to perform a single surprising action. Multiple heads could emerge from Daniel Meader's trick Grand Turk marionette. While the two heads that pop out of the hat had long been known, it was only recently that the third head, emerging from the puppet's stomach, was rediscovered.

Meader's ornately dressed opera singer (opposite) transforms into a hot air balloon when the puppet is flipped over. The balloon, hidden under the puppet's skirts, appears; the head and arms disappear from view; and only the edge of the dress is visible hanging between the balloon and basket.

in *Uncle Tom's Cabin*, an exploding millhouse in *The Miller and His Men*. The English pantomime shows particularly valued huge transformation scenes, for example, when all the characters onstage visibly transformed into *commedia* roles, and the set and plot shifted from a serious story like *Robinson Crusoe* into a spectacular fantasy or "Harlequinade." Such grandiose theatricality challenged the limits of nineteenth-century stage technology. The United States's particular contribution to nineteenth-century spectacle tradition was the minstrel show, which featured white performers like T. D. Rice in blackface, acting out a complicated fear—and

appreciation—of African culture in America. American melodramas also dealt with race, inventing tragically sympathetic Indian characters, like the hero of *Metamora,* at exactly the moment when real Native Americans were facing decimation. Black Americans were played as grateful, God-fearing stereotyped "darkies" in *Uncle Tom's Cabin*, which was the most popular drama of the century. All of these complex images and issues thrived in the performance of American puppet theater.

A good example of this theater was the Royal Marionettes, originally an English troupe started by William Bullock in 1873, which

soon enough spawned a number of competing rivals in England and the United States, all terming themselves one or another variety of "Royal Marionettes." Royal Marionette shows, like those of the Middleton family, featured a variety of different attractions, including "Fantoccini" (an Italian term for trick puppets), minstrel shows, such pantomime extravaganzas as Little Red Riding Hood, and melodramas such as *Babes in the Wood, or, a Mother's Prayer*. In 1876, the founders of one such troupe, McDonough and Earnshaw's Royal Marionettes, met Daniel Meader in San Francisco. Meader, then twenty, was an apprentice theater

prop maker but was hired away by John McDonough and Hartley Earnshaw to speak and sing in their puppet shows—a job considered quite distinct from the work of operating the marionettes. But Meader was fascinated by the challenge of actual puppeteering and secretly taught himself how to manipulate the marionettes. Finally, one night when the chief puppeteer was too drunk to work, Meader stepped in and soon became a puppet operator as well as a singer, performing with the company on its trips across the American continent and around the world.

The Chinaman and the dancing Irish couple (opposite, top) are examples of ethnic and racial stereotypes found in 19th-century shows. While these puppets are from Daniel Meader's variety shows, similar types were used by other puppeteers. The Italian improvisational *commedia dell'arte* played an important part in the development of puppet theater. But the two characters shown here—the dancing Scaramouche and masked Harlequin (opposite, bottom)—found their way into Meader's Punch and Judy shows, a different style of puppet theater.

Daniel Meader (above) and a handbill for a Walter E. Deaves show.

TO-NIGHT! TO-NIGHT!!
FOR A SHORT SEASON ONLY
AT THE
American Cinematograph C
PALACE OF VARIETIES.
51, NORTH SZECHUEN ROAD (NEAR RANGE ROAD.)
WALTER E. DEAVE'S
HIGH CLASS
Vaudeville & Marionette Show

The Success of Two Continents

New York

MANIKIN TRANSFORMATION.
THIS SHOW HAS MADE MILLIONS LAUGH

SPECIAL SCENERY AND ELECTRICAL EFFECTS.
MANIKIN BALLET! HANDSOME COSTUMES

MISS BERYL LYTTON—In Illustrated Songs.
NEW PICTURES! NEW ACTS!!

SEATS BOOKED AT ROBINSON'S PIANO Co. NANKIN ROAD.

In 1882 Meader made his own Royal Marionettes, which reveal his skill as a sculptor and craftsman and provide a good idea of the kind of spectacle presented to audiences. There is a five-member group of black-faced minstrel brass musicians in formal dress, as well as stereotyped "darkies" in workclothes, familiar to the white audiences of *Uncle Tom's Cabin*. Meader created three Chinese characters (perhaps reflecting the large Chinese population in California) with long pigtails as part of his ethnic array, and an Irish "Paddy" character with a green jacket and red hair. Meader's "Grand Turk" (see p. 24) puppet is not so much an ethnic stereotype as an exotic transformation puppet like the English "Grand Turk" mentioned earlier (see p. 18). Meader's marionettes also include such typical pantomime characters as Scaramouche and Harlequin, as well as painted-face clowns, a Punch and Judy set, and some remarkable circus acrobats.

Another California puppeteer, Walter Deaves, had performed Punch and Judy on the streets of San Francisco from the age of fifteen and, in 1874, was also recruited by McDonough and Earnshaw. Like Meader, Deaves later developed his own version of Royal Marionette spectacle, which he called the Marvelous Manikins.

Walter E. Deaves's dancing skeleton (left) could break apart, with each section moving independently of the others before joining back together.

A dramatization of Jules Vernes's *Twenty Thousand Leagues Under the Sea* (opposite, top) was a part of an evening's entertainment at a performance of Walter E. Deaves's troupe. Puppeteer John Lewis included unusual box puppets (opposite, bottom) in his variety shows, although it is not known how he used them. The puppets were apparently seen only from the waist up (they have no legs) and were operated by an internal control system, doing away with the always visible marionette strings.

Deaves's repertoire included the now-traditional minstrel show, featuring a cakewalking couple, as well as *Uncle Tom's Cabin* and a version of Jules Vernes's *Twenty Thousand Leagues Under the Sea*. Clowns and acrobats figured in Deaves's shows, as well as a chorus line of twelve beautiful girls, and a skeleton whose bones could come apart and dance independently of each other.

Deaves also used a particularly interesting and unique form of "box" puppets in his shows, as did one of his contemporaries, John Lewis. These box puppets, apparently visible only from the waist up (they have no legs), sat on a kind of shelf stage, and were operated indirectly by internal control strings attached to the puppets' arms, eyes, and mouth. These hidden mechanisms created a more realistic image of movement than marionettes, whose multiple strings are constantly visible. The puppets' realistically sculpted and painted heads, as well as their colorful costumes—both Deaves's and Lewis's box puppets depict well-dressed, somewhat refined figures—present an immediate, almost startling vision of late-nineteenth-century American character types.

Like Deaves, Lewis also performed marionette variety shows, and his marionettes reflect the nineteenth-century theater's fascination

**J**ohn Lewis's variety shows featured a Chinese dancer, another example of ethnic stereotyping, and a trick clown, whose neck could extend twelve inches above its body.

with transformation and ethnicity. Lewis's puppets include two trick transformation clowns: one with a second hidden head that can sprout out from the first and the other with a telescoping neck, which can suddenly add another twelve inches to the puppet's thirty-inch height. While metamorphoses were a staple of live actors' theater of the time, these particularly extreme transformations could only be performed by puppets—an aspect of the medium that made puppet theater a unique entertainment. Hand in hand with these transformation puppets went such typically unsubtle racial and ethnic stereotypes as a straw-hatted "Chinese Dancer," two grass-skirted "South Sea Dancers," and a brown-skinned "mammy" puppet. These well-constructed and artful marionettes offered puppeteers a certain magnificent distance from reality: the ethnic puppets allowed audiences to consider—or revel in—their sense of the "other"-ness of non-white races without the actual humans in question being present.

Does the connection between transformation and race in Lewis's and most other late nineteenth-century puppets have to do with audiences who are themselves wondering what it means to transform into "Americans"? Certainly puppeteers of the era were conscious of becoming— or trying to become—American.

Many first- or second-generation American puppeteers, such as David Lano and Jesse Jewell, were members of multigenerational European puppet families (see p. 32). David Lano's grandfather Alberto, the son of a street puppeteer in Milan, Italy, arrived in the United States in 1825, and began to perform puppet shows in North and South America with a variety of circuses (including that of the virulently anti-abolitionist comedian Dan Rice). Alberto's son Oliver followed his father's footsteps, traveling by horse and wagon to perform puppet shows—from Punch and Judy to *Faust*—across the United States, even in army camps during the Civil War. The family trade passed on to the next generation as well: Oliver's son David, according to Paul McPharlin, "was born at Irongate, a hamlet between Leesburg and Clifton Forge, Virginia, in 1874, while his parents were traveling in a two-mule van with their puppets and rope-dancing act." This youngest member of the Lano puppet family started his long career at the turn of the century performing in dime museums—spaces devoted to the exhibition of unusual artifacts and theatrical performances—and medicine shows, as his parents and grandfather had. He also performed shadow shows at the 1893 Columbian Exposition in Chicago,

and much later, in 1938, was the director of the Children's Marionette Unit of the Detroit Federal Theater (part of the Works Progress Administration, a national employment program of the Depression era). Ten years after that, at the age of seventy-eight, Lano was still touring, with the Clyde Beatty Circus.

The family of Mae and Jesse Jewell shared a similar history, although they arrived in the United States in 1904, almost eighty years after the Lanos. The Jewells were both puppeteers, with connections to the Holden, Middleton, and McDonough troupes, and created their own company, which performed in American vaudeville houses, dime museums, and circus sideshows (Paul McPharlin saw them perform in Detroit in 1914). Like David Lano, their daughter Lillian was born on the road; she married a vaudeville performer named Rex Faulkner. Their act, Lillian Faulkner and Company, played vaudeville houses until the Depression, using the new technology of the phonograph to provide a soundtrack for their shows.

The English marionette and hand-puppet traditions, which transformed themselves into distinctly American forms, were not the only varieties of European puppet theater to do so. Agrippino Manteo, an orphan in Catania, Sicily, apprenticed with a puppet

Harry Tsouleas's shadow puppets, such as this Greek soldier, inspired Paul McPharlin to include shadow figures in his own work. McPharlin saw Tsouleas, a native of Greece, perform in Detroit coffee houses.

This trick Chinese ball juggler (left) is able to toss the ball up in the air and then balance it on the tip of his toe. The puppet was made by a member of the Lano family. Their family puppet tradition spanned multiple generations, beginning in Italy and then in this country, including performances at army camps during the Civil War and participation in the Federal Theater Project during the Depression.

Jesse Jewell was a member of a multi-generational puppet family with ties to the Royal Marionette troupes in England. This elephant trainer (right) would have been part of the Jewell family's variety show productions, which toured the United States from 1904 through the Depression.

master to learn how to make fifty-pound Sicilian marionettes that could perform *Orlando Furioso* and other epics. Like many young Italians at the turn of the century, Manteo left his native land to find better prospects. He and his wife emigrated to Argentina in 1904, where they performed puppet shows for the large Italian communities of Buenos Aires. After World War I, the Manteos journeyed to New York City, where they joined a handful of other Sicilian puppeteers in Manhattan and Brooklyn. The Manteo family's theater on Manhattan's Lower East Side thrilled audiences with daily installments of the chivalric epics, featuring above all climactic battles in which the metal-clad knights crashed against each other. These performances attracted not only recent Italian immigrants homesick for some familiar entertainment, but also a new generation of American puppeteers, including Remo Bufano and Bil Baird, who thrilled at the theatrical force of this powerful nineteenth-century puppet form. Similarly, the Greek puppeteer Harry Tsouleas was inspired in his native Athens by performances of traditional shadow figures featuring the colorful Greek hero Karaghiosis. After Tsouleas emigrated to Detroit in 1915, he made his own set of fiberboard shadow puppets, which he performed in Detroit coffee houses (see p. 31). In his youth Paul

McPharlin often saw Tsouleas perform, and the Karaghiosis shows later helped inspire McPharlin to incorporate shadow figures in his own puppet work.

Similar transplantations of European traditions took place in Mexico, where the amazingly prolific Aranda family flourished throughout the 1800s and well into the next century. They became something of a national living treasure because of their vivid, extravagant marionette shows, considered "a jewel of realism." During the early 1800s, in the textile-manufacturing town of Huamantla, in the state of Tlaxcala, the brothers Julián and Hermenegildo Aranda were asked by a local priest to create a nativity scene with puppets as part of a church service. Soon joined by two sisters, Ventura and María de la Luz, the brothers created more wooden marionettes for other religious plays, but then branched out from devotional performance to more commercial forms in order to depict all sorts of contemporary Mexican characters on their puppet stage. María de la Luz later married puppeteer Antonio Rosete, after which the troupe became known as the Rosete Aranda company. The detailed, miniature realism of their marionette shows presented brilliant images of rural life, from extravagant village processions celebrating the Immaculate Conception to popular folktales,

## PAUL MCPHARLIN ON GREEK PUPPETEER HARRY TSOULEAS:

"His repertory was inexhaustible, for he improvised upon events from Greek history, current events, and popular narratives. He did an entire evening's show himself, with intervals of rest to take up a collection, speaking the lines for all the characters; a boy assisted him in handing him the figures and putting them away.... Fights—of which there were many... were expressed with terrific din. Shuffling and stamping backstage by the showman and his assistants, the loud whack of a rolled newspaper, the blowing of a whistle, or beating of a drum, to say nothing of hoarse yells, accompanied each fracas. And the more nearly the ceiling was lifted, the better the audience liked it!"

The European marionette tradition flourished in Mexico through the efforts of the Rosete Aranda family, which created these puppets of circus performers. The team of horses is being held back by the circus strongman, while the man at the far right is a trick puppet whose pants repeatedly fall down during the performance.

all at a time when the increasingly rapid growth of cities threatened the very existence of such traditions. But the Aranda troupe's shows, which found appreciative audiences throughout the Americas and on other continents, also reflected images of the new Mexico wrought by urbanism and industrialization. They presented (like their puppeteer neighbors to the north) marionette versions of circus shows and such political spectacles as a procession honoring Mexican independence, featuring six hundred different marionettes (including whole companies of soldiers) and culminating in the appearance of President Porfirio Díaz in a tiny steam-powered car.

Of particular interest is the Rosete Aranda version of the popular character Don Folías, a new, Mexican relative of the Punch, Kasperl, and Guignol characters who served as figures of national identity. Like his European brethren, Don Folías was a recalcitrant troublemaker who made fun of authority, much to the delight of audiences, but to the concern of government authorities trying to censor him— another parallel to the European puppet world. Don Folías's rebellion was not only political and social,

but his phallic nose (in the tradition of puppet tricksters the world over) slyly or overtly suggested the potential for greater sexual transgressions.

The strength of European puppet theater as a tenaciously robust form of popular entertainment influenced the development of puppet theater in North America throughout the nineteenth century. This was a crucial period in which the lines of national and ethnic identities were being defined, not only in politics, philosophy, and literature but also in full color and motion on puppet stages throughout the continent. In the following century, these European traditions would merge with Asian, African, and Native American traditions, as well as new conceptions of machine-age modernity, to create a variety of new "American" forms of puppet theater. ◆

D on Folías was a troublemaker and trickster, not unlike the earlier characters of Punch and Guginol, who served as figures of national identity. This version of the long-nosed character was made by the Mexican Rosete Aranda puppeteer troupe.

This shadow puppet of a demon is
an example of the Indian Tolu
Bommalata puppetry tradition. These
shadow puppets are translucent, casting
richly colored shadows onto the screen.

In Europe and America puppets and masks were relegated to the status of low culture for centuries, but in Asia such theater forms have been considered not only the equals of actors' theater but often one of the highest forms of cultural expression. In India, for example, the interaction of various dramatic forms— ballad singing, recitation, processional theater, cycle plays, mask theater, mask-like make-up, theater, puppet the-figure theater—without or neat categorization the "multiple streams" vastly different perfor- not traditionally low culture, but instead

street theater, temple ater, and shadow-a hierarchical structure has been referred to as of Indian theater. These mance forms were divided into high or were all considered equally viable expressions of Indian stories, beliefs, and aesthetics. In other words, puppet theater was on a cultural parity with all other performance forms. ◆ When Europeans and Americans began to travel to, trade with, battle, and colonize the different regions of India, China, Southeast Asia, and Japan, they inevitably came into contact with highly developed forms of

A "painted face" character, this Chinese marionette (opposite) has fine, articulated fingers, allowing the puppet's hands to open or close. Painted-face figures often portrayed warriors, judges, or outlaws. Marionettes may be the earliest form of Chinese puppet theater.

Traditional Chinese shadow puppet shows feature the favorite gods, warriors, noble ladies, and clowns found in other types of popular theater. The puppets, such as the barbarian general, court lady, and frog demon shown here (below), are made of translucent animal hide and stained with colored dyes. Light passes through the puppets and casts colored shadows onto a screen. The figures are usually controlled by three rods attached to the hands and body, and the puppeteer stands directly behind the figures to press them against the screen.

puppet and mask theater, which—especially in the nineteenth century—they began to document and study. The westerners' understanding of Asian puppet theater (although often inexact or misguided) and the exportation of shadow puppets, rod puppets, hand puppets, and masks to collections in the West greatly influenced the development of western theater throughout the twentieth century. Particular puppet forms from India, Java, China, and Japan—and the sense that they were all valuable currents in the "multiple streams" of Asian theater—opened some westerners' eyes to the possibilities of sophisticated, consistent theater traditions involving puppets, thus confirming these westerners' belief that puppetry could be a powerful means of creating modern theater. As late as 1950, for example, well-known Chicago television

puppeteer Burr Tillstrom suggested that the cultural importance which puppet theater traditionally held in Asia offered a model for contemporary American society. In order to articulate his desire to create a serious, adult puppet theater, he approvingly offered the example of "ancient Chinese and other orientals" who "used puppets and shadow figures in religious plays and pageants."

Three things tend to characterize Asian puppet theater. First of all, Asian puppet theaters are often the visual means of performing the most valued stories in a particular community and consequently are of central importance to the artistic, cultural, and social identity of those groups. Second, although in the West most performance culture has been effectively separated from religious function since the

Renaissance, Asian puppet forms still retain essential connections to religious and spiritual beliefs and powers. And third, puppet shows in Asia are very often presented in the context of community ritual, not simply as commercial entertainment. All of these aspects of Asian puppet theater offered a bracing and thought-provoking contrast to the situation of puppet theater in the West.

## CHINESE PUPPET THEATERS

It was with a sense of these aspects of Asian puppet theater that Paul McPharlin asked his colleague Benjamin March, a curator at the Detroit Institute of Arts, to collect shadow figures for him during March's 1931 trip to Peking. As a result, the museum has a complete set of shadow figures, scenery, properties, and scripts used by a traveling Chinese troupe during the early twentieth century.

Chinese shadow theater (termed *pi-ying xi*, or "theater of lantern shadows") has existed in almost every province of China since at least the eleventh century B.C. Originally performed on street corners and marketplaces, shadow shows featured the favorite gods, warriors, scholars, noble ladies, servants, and clowns that figured in other forms of popular Chinese theater. Beginning in the Sung dynasty (A.D. 960–1279) shadow players were also paid to perform in the courtyards of family houses—

private shows that could last from noon to midnight. Like puppet forms the world over, the popularity of Chinese shadow theater suffered greatly following the introduction of cinema in the early twentieth century. Yet, like other puppet traditions in Asia, Chinese shadow theater has persisted through means of government support and various efforts to "modernize" the form and content of its repertoire.

Traditional Chinese shadow figures are made of translucent donkey hide, cowhide, or pigskin. Their shapes are cut out with sharp knives, and the figures stained with black, red, green, blue, or yellow dyes. The translucent nature of the puppets allows the light to pass through the figures, taking on the colors of the various dyes, and casting colored shadows on the screen. Chinese shadow troupes used to feature one central puppeteer, although during the twentieth century multiple performers became more common. The figures are usually controlled by three rods attached by flexible joints to the puppet's body and hands, thus allowing the puppeteer standing directly behind them to press the puppets against a portable screen. A light mounted at the height of the puppeteer's head throws the puppets' shadows on the screen. Removable heads allow puppeteers some mix-and-match possibilities in character creation, although such variations are limited. Like other forms of classic Chinese theater, Chinese shadow puppet shows adhere to a tradition of clearly defined character types who are instantly identifiable by facial features, costume designs, colors, and characteristic gestures. Performances are marked by dialogue and sung recitation, accompanied by music played on the *hu ch'in* (a bowed string instrument), gongs, and other traditional instruments of Chinese theater. The stories presented in Chinese shadow shows range from episodes of classic Chinese epics such as *Romance of the Three Kingdoms* to folklore and contemporary tales, handed down orally or passed on by written scripts.

The shadow figures acquired for Paul McPharlin were used for a light-hearted trilogy of short plays featuring Kung-Tzu, the lovesick

Paul McPharlin demonstrates a Chinese shadow theater performance, using puppets now in the collection bearing his name. The puppet hanging below the screen at the far left is probably Te-Yung on a bicycle (opposite).

son of a rich man; his servant Te-Yung; the magical White Fox, who bewitches Kung-Tzu and can transform into any character; and Chung K'uei, an exorcist who finally frees the young man after an exciting battle. The figures in this group typify the aesthetics of Chinese shadow theater because of their mix of realism and fantasy, their consistent play with and against verisimilitude. The many set pieces present detailed representations of traditional Chinese furniture, household objects, vehicles, and architecture, but these are played off the White Fox's many fantastic transformations. In the play *Visting Li Er Ssu*, the traditional characters Kung-Tzu and Te-Yung ride modern bicycles and are met at a temple by a policeman in modern western-style dress. Such juxtapositions have been central to Chinese performance traditions for centuries, but in the West in the twentieth century they were considered examples of avant-garde aesthetics.

Marionettes may represent the earliest form of Chinese puppet theater. By the time of the T'ang dynasty (A.D. 618–906) Chinese marionette theater had become a sophisticated art form and yet retained its connections to the spirit world and folk religion. According to Roberta Stalberg, a historian of Chinese puppet

**A** Chinese puppeteer blended the old and the new in this shadow figure. Te-Yung, a traditional character from the centuries-old shadow theater repertoire, is riding a modern bicycle.

theater, Chinese folk beliefs "pictured the world as crowded with spirits, ready to do good or evil as the mood took them." Such spirit forces, usually up to mischief more than benevolence, "were quick to inhabit any object open to their possession, and puppets, having human shape, were especially desirable." Marionette theaters particularly thrived in Fujian and Quanzhou provinces in southeastern China, where such puppet performances functioned not only as entertainment but as part of weddings, birthdays, funerals, and exorcism rites. Like Chinese shadow theater, Chinese marionette performances traditionally featured a small orchestra, sung texts, and the same type of characters found in Peking opera: male, or *sheng*, roles; female, or *dan*, characters; *bei* characters such as warriors, judges, and outlaws, also known as "painted face" roles because of the elaborate and fantastic makeup decorating the figures' faces (see p. 39); and miscellaneous, or *za*, character types. Chinese marionettes have traditionally differed from their European counterparts in terms of the number of strings used to operate them. While European marionettes usually have been controlled by anywhere from two to eight strings, Chinese marionettes typically have sixteen strings on average, but sometimes as many

Japanese Bunraku puppets are operated by three puppeteers in full view of the audience. The three performers, each responsible for moving a portion of the figure, must act in unison to manipulate the puppet in a realistic manner. A narrator, or *joruri*, seated by the side of the stage, recites all of the dialogue. This pair of puppets, a beautiful lady and a Samurai warrior, were probably used in the same performance. The Samurai carries a sword, appropriate for the many battle scenes in Bunraku theater, and has moveable eyes and eyebrows.

as thirty-two, a difference allowing minute articulation of the puppets' limbs.

China is also the home of the most dexterously manipulated hand puppets in the world, part of a tradition centered in Fujian province, and said to have emerged in the sixteenth century. Chinese puppeteers are famous for making their hand puppets dance, juggle, and perform such acrobatic feats as leaping out of windows (as the puppeteer expertly tosses them from one hand to another), skills unknown in western hand puppet traditions. The characters follow the same design codes marking other forms of Chinese puppet and actors' theater, including *sheng* and *bei* figures.

## JAPAN

Japanese puppet traditions are known in the West mostly through the form of Bunraku, whose puppets are operated by three puppeteers in full view of the audience. The French dramatist Paul Claudel saw Bunraku performances in Japan in the 1920s and was transfixed by the form and the way the puppeteers—working with a narrator and musician—moved the puppets in space. The Bunraku puppet, Claudel wrote, "has no contact with earth, and moves with equal ease in all dimensions. It floats in an intangible element like a drawing in empty space. Its life is in its

center, and its four limbs and head, spread out like rays around it, are merely its elements of expression. It is a talking star, untouchable." Chikamatsu Monzaemon, considered by some to be Japan's greatest playwright, wrote exquisitely plotted tragedies of middle-class life for the Bunraku stage in the late seventeenth and early eighteenth centuries, dramas whose realism is matched with the sense of ritual action and spirituality found in other Asian puppet forms.

## INDIA

The many different cultures and societies of the Indian subcontinent have produced rich and tremendously varied forms of puppet and object theater. Some of the oldest living traditions of theater in the world, these types of theater

These Indian puppets are all kings or high-ranking courtiers, including some with characteristic forehead markings designating their social positions. Known as Kathputli marionettes (Kathputli means "wooden doll"), the puppets have wooden heads, while their bodies and arms are made of stuffed cloth. Kathputli troupes perform shows centered around tales of valor, romance, and warfare among warrior-kings in medieval times.

The Tolu Bommalata shadow figures in the McPharlin Collection, such as this turbaned figure, depict characters from the *Ramayana*, one of India's two great Sanskrit epics.

influenced performance forms throughout the rest of Asia. Indian shadow puppet theaters present scenes from the country's two great Sanskrit epics, the *Ramayana* and *Mahabharata*, in performances that are as much religious ritual as entertainment. The episodes from the epics may be told over a series of consecutive nighttime performances and tend to focus on popular crowd pleasers, especially battle scenes. Tolu Bommalata shadow figures, a southern Indian tradition from the state of Andhra Pradesh, are large (see pp. 36, 44). Like their Chinese counterparts, they are translucent, allowing rich colors to fill the screen.

As with many forms of puppet theater, these Indian shadow figures are performed in combination with songs, recitation, and instrumental music. Conventional song structures help the puppeteers recall specific sung poems, and spoken lines are improvised according to oral tradition. A skilled puppeteer can make cross references among a variety of local and national epics. Tolu Bommalata performers are usually family groups, often including a husband, wife, and children, which used to travel throughout Andhra Pradesh, setting up their portable stages in various local villages. Over the course of the twentieth century many such wandering puppeteers settled in different places throughout the region, but

ceasing their peripatetic lifestyle did not make their puppeteering more secure. Film and television, as they have everywhere else in the world, created strong competition for the old forms of puppet theater. Concerted efforts by the Indian government support the continuation of these traditional puppet theaters.

The Kathputli marionettes of Rajasthan (see p. 45), in northwest India, feature a very simple method of string operation: the puppeteer holds two looped strings, one running from the puppet's head to its torso, and the other connecting the puppet's two hands. Kathputli means "wooden doll," and the heads of these puppets are indeed carved out of wood, while their bodies and down-turned arms are stuffed cloth. Such simple design and control does not prevent these puppets from being capable of a variety of movements, including walking, running, dancing, or fighting. Kathputli troupes perform on a floor-level cloth stage with a backdrop suggesting the arcade of a palace. The puppets' movements are accompanied by drums and the sounds of a bamboo and leather reed that the main puppeteer holds in his mouth, a relative of the "swazzle" long employed by hand puppet performers in Europe.

A related form of Indian performance is called *pår*, which uses

The *Ramayana*, composed in the third century B.C., relates the adventures of the king Rama, who is deprived of his throne and exiled with his wife Sita. After Sita is abducted by a demon king, Rama allies himself with Sugriva, the monkey king, and Hanuman, a monkey general, who aid him in a great battle in Lanka (Sri Lanka). At the battle's end, Rama frees Sita and regains his kingdom. The *Mahabharata*, a later work composed between 200 B.C. and 200 A.D., is the longest work in world literature. It depicts a fabulous dynastic struggle and civil war between the Pendawa and Kurawa families in the kingdom of Kurukshetra. It features such characters as Arjuna, Krishna, Bima, and the Pendawa queen Drupadi.

painted pictures to tell its stories rather than articulated puppets. The centuries-old *pår* tradition continues in Rajasthan, where its stories are often performed for hours into the night by a narrator (or *bhopo*) and his assistant (two men or a husband-and-wife team), who alternate between chanted recitation and song. The narrator points to the relevant parts of the tale depicted on the painting, improvising that evening's story structure as he performs, while his assistant illuminates the images with a lamp. The stories are epic tales of Rajput warrior kings, the most famous of whom is Pabuji. The narrator is actually a kind of shaman (a lay priest with functional connections to the spiritual world), and the painting itself is akin to a portable shrine.

## JAVA

Some of the oldest existing traditions of puppet theater in the world come from Java, the central island of Indonesia. The various forms of puppet and puppet-related performance there are all termed *wayang*, which can be translated as "shadow"—an indication of the pre-eminence of shadow theater. Unlike Chinese shadow figures, which play with the possibilities of colored light, Javanese puppets are opaque, allowing no light to pass through and casting an entirely black shadow. Similar to Chinese puppet theater, however, Javanese

puppet performances have retained a central connection to family and community rituals, and while they can be immensely funny and up to date, at the same time they are also serious and highly traditional. They offer a strong connection between long-ago Javanese history and the present, functioning as an integral aspect of modern Javanese life. Javanese theater operates simultaneously on different levels— as entertainment, community activity, and devotional act. The complexities and happy contradictions of Javanese theater, such as the Hindu tales performed by largely Muslim puppeteers, offer examples of how apparently "simple" forms of puppet and object theater can contain immense and intriguing challenges.

The epics of Javanese theater are for the most part based on the two great Hindu epics from India, the *Ramayana* and the *Mahabharata*, transformed into Javanese contexts and combined with native Javanese epics. Traditionally, *wayang* shadow theater performances often take place as part of a ritual exorcism, or other community ceremony, and can last as long as nine hours, starting in the evening and ending the next morning.

The characters of *wayang* performances remain consistent in all of the puppet forms: heroes and villains of two warring families, gods and demi-gods that populate this world, and divine clowns, who

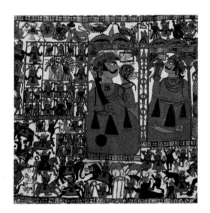

The Indian performance form known as *pår* uses painted pictures to tell its stories. Narration is provided by two people using chanted recitation and song.

All Javanese puppet forms are called *wayang*, meaning shadow, attesting to the pre-eminence of shadow theater in Java. The characters of all the *wayang* performances remain constant: heroes, villains, gods, and divine clowns. Javanese shadow puppets (above), called *wayang kulit,* are made of leather and are opaque. No light passes through them, so they cast solid black shadows. *Wayang kletek* rod puppets (above, right) are made of wood, carved in a low-relief style. They are performed without a shadow screen, making the painted decorations and clothing visible to the audience. *Wayang golek* figures (right) are fully three-dimensional. Their control system allows for expressive movements and poses.

participate in and outrageously comment on the actions. A sophisticated language of character types allows audiences to instantly recognize heroes, villains, gods, and clowns as soon as they appear onstage, according to their size, form, color, ornamentation, and carving. Characters embodying ideal qualities tend to be small and elegant; those representing undesirable traits are large (sometimes enormous), muscular, and hairy. What makes *wayang* compelling is that its characters exist along many different points between these two extremes, combining various degrees of both in fascinating complexity.

*Wayang kulit* (kulit means "leather") is probably the most well known of Javanese puppet forms (see p. 47, top). It features flat, intricately cut out leather shadow figures operated by means of a buffalo-horn rod extending below the puppet's body, and usually with two more rods to control the puppet's articulated arms. *Wayang kulit* shadow-puppet shows are performed by one person, the *dalang*, who is not only a puppeteer but playwright, orchestra conductor, and shaman. Music for *wayang kulit* performances is traditionally played by a gamelan, the Javanese classical orchestra of tuned percussive gong instruments, drums, and singers. The *dalang* provides voices in addition to the puppets' movements and improvises the performance of excerpts from Javanese epics according to fixed rhythms and tonal forms passed down from generation to generation.

*Wayang kletek* rod puppets retain the flat profile of the leather shadow figures but are carved from wood in a low relief style that takes advantage of the three-dimensional possibilities of the medium (see p. 47, top). They are performed without a shadow screen, above a curtain that hides the puppeteer. *Wayang golek* figures, although also carved from wood, are fully three-dimensional rod puppets. A central control rod passes up through a wooden shoulder yoke to connect to the puppet's head (which is hinged to allow for up-and-down movement). The puppet's arms, connected to the moveable shoulder piece, are controlled by two additional rods. This system allows for a whole range of expressive body movements and positions. *Wayang beber* presents the same kinds of stories and characters as other forms of *wayang*, but as pictures painted on a long scroll rolled around two staffs and performed as a kind of moving panorama. The form is similar to Indian *pår* paintings, but with the added element of movement as the pictures are advanced.

## THAILAND

The *nang talung* shadow theater tradition from the south of Thailand is similar to the Javanese leather *wayang kulit* form: the puppets are operated from below by a single vertical rod, which is often augmented by an articulated arm. Traditionally accompanied by an orchestra of drums, gongs, cymbals, and stringed instruments, *nang talung* performances feature stories of gods, demons, and mortal Thai characters. Some stories are based on the *Ramkien*, the Thai version of the *Ramayana*, while others tell more local or modern tales.

A nineteenth-century set of leather *nang talung* characters features a wide array of male and female clowns (*talok)*, a dragon (*naga)*, demons with tails, and a nicely perforated warrior god, but the human characters, unlike Javanese shadow figures, appear in modern, not traditional dress. This is also true of a twentieth-century set of *nang talung* figures, which are additionally remarkable because they are made not of leather but of newspaper—an interesting example of modern mass-media being recycled into a traditional puppet form.

These are *nang talung* shadow puppets from Thailand. They are similar to Javanese *wayang kulit* puppets in that both are made of leather, are opaque, and cast solid black shadows.

The Turkish shadow theater known as Karagöz (named for its central character) dates back to the sixteenth century. Historians believe its origins might be found in Asian shadow forms such as *wayang kulit*, which Arab traders may have carried westward, although connections to Egyptian shadow figures and the Italian *commedia dell'arte* tradition are also suspected. Although clear cultural connections are always hard to prove, Karagöz shadow theater shares characteristics with puppet forms on two continents, particularly in its focus on the irreverent, bawdy, local culture hero and trickster Karagöz who propels each comic episode.

This double puppet of the Turkish character Karagöz and his friend Haçivat depicts the two in a rowboat. It is a scene from a play called *The Boat*, in which the pair, unemployed and deserted by their wives, try to make a living by ferrying a variety of characters across the Bosphorus straits.

Karagöz puppets, like Chinese and Indian shadow figures, are translucent and colored, and like the Chinese ones, they are also operated by rods attached perpendicular to the figures. Karagöz theater, like many other puppet forms, is based on broad, archetypal characters, in this case representing the variety of ethnicities and nationalities present in Istanbul at the height of the Ottoman Empire. The stylized leather puppets are usually performed by a solo puppeteer who reads from a script backstage, speaking all the voices and singing songs. Karagöz (the word literally means "black eye," a distinguishing feature of the puppet) is the central character, a kind of ribald everyman and resident of Istanbul, similar in demeanor to the English puppet Punch. Karagöz exchanges repartée with his comrade and foil Haçivat, and the two pursue comic and often risqué adventures in various corners of Istanbul, meeting a variety of different characters on the street, in bathhouses, brothels, and coffeehouses.

Europeans and Americans gradually came to learn more about Asian puppet theater during the twentieth century, and differences in social and cultural context—as well as more obvious differences

of technique—had a great effect on western puppet theaters. Japanese forms like Bunraku boldly contradicted western notions of realism and the supposed necessity of hiding the puppet's operation. At the same time, the acute detail—or super-realism—of Chinese hand puppet performance was leaps and bounds beyond what the most skilled western puppeteers could do. In addition, Chinese, Javanese, Thai, and Indian shadow theater forms showed westerners examples of highly refined, non-realistic projected images that could be used to retell the most central stories of a given culture.

The most important lessons westerners learned from Asian puppet theater had to do with the place of such theater in Asian culture. Not simply a form of entertainment, and hardly limited to children's audiences, Asian puppet theaters were clearly at the center of Asian performance cultures, not peripheral or "low-culture," as they seemed to be in the West. Equally important was the fact that most Asian theater forms, including puppet theaters, so clearly maintained a direct connection to spirituality and religion, something that the West had been attempting to avoid for centuries. ◆

Turkish shadow puppets, like those of China and India, are translucent, letting light filter through to cast colored shadows. The central character of Turkish shadow theater is Karagöz, an irreverent, bawdy trickster not unlike the English Punch. He is depicted here at left, with his oversize arm, facing a watchman carrying a lantern.

In her 1937 production of *Death of Tintagiles*, Marjorie Batchelder used rod puppets, a relatively novel puppet technique in the United States at that time. The puppets are closer in design to three-dimensional Javanese rod puppets than to popular European traditions, an indication of the international character of modern puppetry. Shown here (from left to right) are the characters Algovale, Ygraine, and Tintagiles.

The birth of modern American puppet theater dates to the early twentieth century. The sense that the twentieth century would redefine the concept of "modern" had its roots in European cultural currents of the nineteenth century, which sought to temper the seemingly inexorable development of the West as an industrial, urban society based on realism, rationalism, and capitalism. There was a search for and idealization of traces of the non-rational, the non-realistic, the non-western, and the pre-industrial as a kind of spiritual salve for the inexorable hardness of the encroaching machine age. Beginning with the Romantics in the

early 1800s, who saw emotion and intuition as the equal of reason; continuing through such developments as the Arts and Crafts Movement, which championed the role of traditional crafts in an age of industrial design; and culminating with the late-nineteenth century Symbolists, who emphasized interior states of mind over naturalism; writers, philosophers, and artists began to respond to the modern age with artistic methods and theories that inevitably (and perhaps

contradictorily) combined technological achievements with ancient
aesthetics. Puppet theater was
central to such experiments, from
Heinrich von Kleist's metaphysical
treatise *On the Marionette Theater*
in 1810 to Alfred Jarry's outrageous
assertions (with his 1896 play *Ubu
Roi*) that puppetry should be the
model for all modern theater. Jarry
was not alone in his turn-of-the-
century rediscovery of puppet theater. Maurice Maeterlinck, Arthur
Schnitzler, William Butler Yeats,
Hugo von Hofmannsthal, Paul
Claudel, and other Symbolist playwrights also saw a kind of artistic
truth in the physicality of marionettes and masks—especially in
the face of the astounding realism
becoming possible through
photography and film.

The western rediscovery of
puppet theater in the early twentieth
century—or its "revival" as Paul
McPharlin put it—began in Europe
and involved a number of factors:
a newfound valuation of the traditionally low-culture art of European
puppet theater; an appreciation of
Asian, African, and Native American
puppet performance as models for
western artists; a renewed sense
of puppet theater not only as commercial entertainment but as a
cultural, spiritual, and educational
element; and a sense that these
older practices and purposes of
puppet theater could be pragmati-
cally combined with any machine
age innovations yet to come. This

is not to say that all modernist
puppeteers agreed with each other
about what twentieth-century
puppet theater should be; but they
all had a sense of new and exciting
possibilities for this centuries-old
art form.

The primary European exponent
of modern puppet theater as a
legitimate art form equal or superior
to actors' theater was the English
artist, actor, director, and writer
Edward Gordon Craig. Craig was
not unusual in proposing a romantic
alternative to the mass, industrialized culture developing across
western Europe and (especially)
in the United States, but he was a
bit uncommon in espousing non-
realistic, ritualized performance
with masks and puppets as the
"theater of the future."

Throughout the early twentieth
century, a succession of avant-garde
movements in different European
countries—Futurism, Expressionism,
Dada, Constructivism, the Bauhaus—
all followed Symbolism's effort to
define modern culture specifically
through art and performance. As
modern industrial societies created
that culture, with or without those
movements' assistance, the United
States was a constant image of
what modernity looked like. So it
is only fitting that American puppet
theater of the early twentieth century fulfilled a variety of modernist
ambitions, and that Paul McPharlin,
a puppeteer from the United States's
most important industrial city,

Detroit, would be at the center of
that modernism.

Puppet theater did not re-emerge
simply in the arena of educated
western artists. Equally modern
were the ways in which highly traditional popular art forms adapted
themselves to and reflected change
in the societies in which they existed. After all, an ability to adapt to
changing circumstances was a
necessary survival method for such
living art forms. We have seen
how nineteenth-century dress and
machines could be reflected in the
apparently rigid and centuries-old
image system of Chinese shadow
theater (see p. 41). Similar reflec-
tions of modern change could be
found in the appearance of western
clothing on Javanese *wayang golek*
puppets. The McPharlin Collection
also has some interesting examples
of Japanese hand puppets created
by K. Udriyama in the 1930s.
These puppets, although they represent traditional characters, are
created in a form and style different
from the traditional design aesthetics of Japanese puppet forms of
Bunraku and rod puppet theater—
almost as if they reflected the
aesthetics of western realism.

A different kind of adaptation
occurred throughout Europe in
the early decades of the century
as artists turned to traditional
European puppet forms in order
to pursue new purposes. This was
the case in Russia, after the 1917
Revolution, which energized a

This pair of unpainted papier-mâché marionettes, a queen and a dancer, were built by puppet innovator Michael Carmichael Carr for director Edward Gordon Craig and show a typically modern combination of interests. Abstract geometrical forms are visible in the torsos and limbs, while the faces and headwear reflect Asian design motifs.

generation of modern Russian artists to apply the radical aesthetics of Futurism and Constructivism to the creation of a modern revolutionary society. Toward this end young artists turned to the traditions of Petrushka hand puppet theater, first as a means of spreading the revolution, and later as a method of mass education. The recalcitrant underdog Petrushka was a hero of popular theater, a working-class trickster in continual conflict with authority—a perfect revolutionary, it would seem.

A "Red Petrushka" collective began in 1927; the "Red Army Petrushka Group" started the next year, and various other Petrushka companies sprang up in factory clubs. All of these groups, according to a Soviet historian, "carried out idiosyncratic and extremely useful educational work in schools, clubs, and pioneer camps." The use of traditional Russian puppet theater for education and propaganda was relatively well known in the United States, in part because of McPharlin's 1935 English translation of *The Adventures of a Russian Puppet Theatre* by Nina Efimova. Efimova was a visual artist who, together with her architect husband Ivan Efimov, adapted the techniques of the fairground Petrushka theaters to perform short hand-puppet plays like *How a Peasant Fed Two Generals* in factories, clubs, libraries, theaters, barns, barracks, union halls, railroad stations, parks, business co-operatives, and hospitals in provinces as well as in big cities. One of the most important aspects of the Red Petrushka theaters is that the title character's eternal problem with any authority soon led the Soviet state to suppress the rebellious and anarchic Petrushka in favor of a more benign and bland Petrushka, whose main purpose was to educate children. This conception of the form and purpose of puppet theater came to epitomize the active state-supported puppet theater in Eastern Bloc countries during the Cold War, but it also had clear parallels in children's-oriented puppet theater in the West, which became equally devoted to the tasks of education and advertising—the western version of propaganda.

## PUPPET VISIONARIES AND THE NEW WORLD

In the first decade of the new century, a California painter, Michael Carmichael Carr, and his Dutch wife worked with Edward Gordon Craig in Italy, as Craig experimented with new staging and lighting designs. Carr built scale-model sets for Craig, and his wife translated Dutch documentations of Javanese *wayang* performance, which texts Craig would later use in his magazines *The Mask* and *The Marionette*.

Carr built a number of unpainted papier-maché marionettes (see p. 55) for Craig that show a typically modern combination of interests: abstract geometrical form (in the torso and limbs) and Asian design motifs (in the head and headdress). Of course, the whole idea that "experiments" in some kind of scientific method might be conducted in puppet or any other type of theater was also a modern concept. Carr later made more such puppets for Cleveland puppeteer Helen Haiman Joseph, who popularized Craig's concepts of puppet theater in her 1920 *Book of Marionettes*.

In a way, the strongest impression Craig's theater ideas made in the United States was in the Midwest. Carr seems to have worked there after his experience in Italy, and scenic designer Samuel Hume, an early and important Craig collaborator, pursued his own work in Detroit upon his return from abroad. McPharlin himself corresponded with Craig with some frequency and was clearly inspired by the letters Craig sent him. These included Craig's idealized expectations for puppet theater, as articulated in a 1933 letter to McPharlin: "Puppetry is a true art—the true art of the theatre-in-little, theatricals having got their deserts and become a false kind of photography enlarged."

The rediscovery of puppet theater represented an aspect of artistic regeneration for modern European artists and audiences, and in the Craig/Carr connection it found open and receptive ears in the New World. But puppet modernism meant something quite different in the United States, where the oldest theater traditions were Native American performance forms, the commercial showmanship of melodrama, circus, minstrelsy, and vaudeville, and the quasi-underground array of African-American performance forms of dance, music, and theater. Most of the Americans involved in American puppet modernism were not yet ready to attempt an understanding of Native American culture; continued to see African-American forms through the haze of nineteenth-century racism and paternalism; and felt ambivalent about commercial theater traditions focused solely on entertainment and the bottom line of economic success. Inspired by the stirring (and often utopian) ideals of the European avant-garde, modernist American puppeteers wanted to create new forms of puppet theater that would answer social, political, educational, and economic needs in the twentieth-century democracy of the United States. In other words, they wanted to create modern puppet theater as an art form fully integrated into American society. The shift, as puppeteer Bil Baird put it, was from the "traditionalism" and "vaudeville tricks" of the "wandering showmen"

These two papier-mâché Red Petrushka hand puppets are rare evidence of a mixture of traditional puppet theater and revolution. Following the 1917 Russian Revolution to overthrow the czar, artists turned to the traditional hand puppet Petrushka as a means of communinication and education for the masses. Petrushka, on the right, is dressed in peasant clothes as is the woman beside him.

to "a new premise— that the best puppetry derived from the highest artistic and creative effort."

The elevated and somewhat ambiguous goals Baird defines could obviously be interpreted a number of different ways, and they were. Modernist American puppeteers in the early twentieth century engaged in a wide variety of significant cultural projects. Although they saw puppet theater's value as a highly entertaining and effective medium of show business, they also considered it a serious art form suitable for the performance of classic dramatic texts of high cultural value. It was also seen as a means of enriching different forms of education, therapy, and recreation; and as a means of engaging in the persuasive performance discourses of politics or advertising products to a growing consumer society. Some American puppeteers in the early twentieth century focused on one or two particular aspects of these wide-ranging goals, while others sought to explore the full range of possibilities now apparently available to them. Paul McPharlin termed this nexus of new puppet theater methods "the artistic puppetry revival," and wrote that "by 1915 American amateurs were thinking seriously of the aesthetic and educative possibilities of puppetry." By 1920, he continued, "they had brought about a revival of puppetry as an artistic medium and explored new applications for it."

## PUPPET MODERNISM AND THE LITTLE THEATER MOVEMENT

The birth of modernism in American theater as a whole—not only in puppet theater—started in the Midwest, when Maurice Browne and Ellen Van Volkenburg founded the Chicago Little Theater in 1912. This soon gave rise to a nationwide Little Theater Movement, inspiring the creation of community playhouses "dedicated to theater art rather than business," as historian John Gassner put it. The Provincetown Playhouse in New York City was part of this movement, and Eugene O'Neill emerged from it to invent modern American drama as an art form respected around the world. But puppet theater was also central to the Little Theater Movement's goals, beginning with Volkenburg, who explored the medium as a way of presenting traditional stories on stage. Volkenburg studied European marionette traditions and adapted them to perform her own plays (such as *The Deluded Dragon*) as well as Shakespeare's *A Midsummer Night's Dream.* Typical of the new puppet modernism, Volkenburg was not a member of a puppeteering family, nor did she apprentice to an established puppeteer; instead she examined existing traditions and invented her own versions of them, starting from the ground

up and making her own mistakes as she refined her performance medium.

Volkenburg's ventures into puppet theater (which, incidentally, even included the invention of the term "puppeteer") were paralleled in another midwestern Little Theater, the Cleveland Playhouse, where Helen Haiman Joseph began experimenting with puppets in 1915 with a shadow-theater production of William Butler Yeats's *Shadowy Waters.* In addition to her support of Michael Carmichael Carr and her articulation of the high goals of European puppet modernism through her *Book of Marionettes,* Joseph continued to mine the literature of the European symbolists with a production of Maeterlinck's *Death of Tintagiles* in 1916. In addition she also directed her puppet company in such traditional folktales as *Sleeping Beauty* and in her productions of Shakespeare plays.

The modernist puppet movement in New York City was really initiated by Tony Sarg, a puppeteer and illustrator of German heritage, born in Guatemala in 1880. He lived for a brief spell in London, where he learned how to make and operate marionettes by watching the traditional nineteenth-century variety theater performances of the Thomas Holden company. He later wrote: "I followed Holden from theater to theater and saw forty-eight performances from the

Tony Sarg, an early force in the modernist puppet movement, is shown with a marionette, probably a character from a production of *The Wind in the Willows.*

Tony Sarg's marionettes for his 1939 production of Robin Hood demonstrate his sense of dramatic color and exotic action. Robin Hood, with bow in hand, and one of his Merry Men stand by Maid Marion, seated on the horse.

Remo Bufano created puppets based on characters from a popular 1932 comic strip, *The Little King*. This marionette (opposite) is The Other King.

front row, where I could peer up inside the masking of the stage. I saw the type of controllers used. I noticed that the marionettes were very flexible at the waist, like hollow stockings. And I learned much besides." Sarg arrived in New York in 1915 and began to produce marionette shows for friends at his studio in the Flatiron Building on Broadway. The success of these performances led him to produce more formal shows at the Neighborhood Playhouse (a fixture of the Little Theater Movement), and to recruit a company of puppeteers to construct puppets, write scripts, manage, and perform the mixture of classic fairy tales and European literature that came to typify his work. Sarg learned about effective dramatic structure and

various puppet construction techniques from Ellen Van Volkenburg, who came from Chicago in 1919 to direct Sarg's production of *The Rose and the Ring* (adapted from William Makepeace Thackeray's original story by another Chicago Little Theater puppeteer, Hettie Louise Mick). He also sought and received advice from Helen Haiman Joseph. As a result of his canny new approach to puppetry as art theater, Sarg's productions, according to Paul McPharlin, marked a substantial departure from the nineteenth-century traditions of European marionette theater, setting up "an ideal for American puppetry: a good play, as a rule based on a familiar tale, with all production details carefully worked out and integrated." In Sarg's shows, McPharlin wrote, "puppets, scenery, lights, properties, and even the printed programs, exhibited artistry."

Sarg's enterprise grew into a substantial production company, and for two decades scores of young puppeteers (including Lilian Owen Thompson, Sue Hastings, Bil Baird, and Rufus Rose) got their first training in the field on Sarg's cross-country tours. Sarg concentrated on marionettes but explored shadow theater in his 1924 production of *The Chinese Willow Plate Story*. Sarg designed large puppet spectacles for the A&P supermarket chain at the 1933 Chicago World's Fair—an early

example of the profitable connection between puppets and advertising—and also designed many figures for department store window displays. Perhaps most spectacularly, Sarg was responsible for designing the first inflatable puppets for the Thanksgiving Day parades organized by Macy's department store in New York City (see p. 8).

Remo Bufano was a rough-and-tumble puppeteer a few years younger than Sarg. His ideas were usually big, bold, and expressive, in contrast to Sarg's careful attention to detail and organization. Born in Italy, Bufano grew up in New York's Greenwich Village with fourteen brothers and sisters. The traditional Sicilian marionette theaters then active in New York's Italian neighborhoods had a strong early influence on him. Performances of the *Orlando Furioso* epic, full of knights, beautiful warrior maidens, battles, romance, sorcerers, betrayal, and outspokenly didactic portrayals of great moral and religious conflicts inspired the adolescent Bufano to create his own version of the puppet show at home and provided an introduction to the art that would become the focus of his life.

During the years 1910-19, Bufano, then in his twenties, became intimately involved with the early efforts of the Little Theater Movement and acted and worked backstage with the Washington Square Players, the Provincetown Players, and the politically radical New Playwrights Theater. Bufano also continued making and performing puppet shows of his own; he and his wife Florence performed *Orlando Furioso* (1922) and works from the early modern repertoire of puppet art theater, such as Edna St. Vincent Millay's *Two Slatterns and a King* (1922) and Arthur Schnitzler's *Gallant Cassian* (1923), for both humble and sophisticated audiences.

Bufano developed his repertoire of marionette and hand-puppet shows at the Provincetown Playhouse and, after 1926, in his own studio theater on West 12th Street. The wide variety of these productions included such fairy tales as *The Fisherman and His Wife*, the traditional *Tragedy of Mr. Punch*, and contemporary pieces like *The Big Fight*, which featured two modern boxers. In response to the emerging mass-media popularity of the comic strip, he created puppets based on characters from *The Little King* (1932) strip, and even a hand puppet Purimspiel (a play for the Jewish holiday of Purim), called *In Shushan the Capital*, a retelling of the traditional Purim story of the Jewish queen Esther, the Persian king Ahasuerus, and the struggle of Esther and her cousin Mordecai to prevent the evil courtier Haman from massacring the Jews (see p. 62). For *Fantasy in Flutes and Figures*, a 1926 play

In *Shushan the Capital*, a Purimspiel, Remo Bufano used hand puppets to retell the story of the Jewish holiday Purim, in which the Jewish queen Esther (center) and her cousin Mordecai (right) convince the Persian king Ahasuerus (left) to spare the life of the country's Jews.

Remo Bufano created full body suits, worn by the puppeteer, for the Walrus and the Carpenter (below) from a popular 1932 production of *Alice in Wonderland*. Bufano based the puppets on Sir John Tenniel's original illustrations published in the Lewis Carroll book.

by New Playwrights Theater member Em Jo Basshe, Bufano built a series of abstract marionettes representing algebraic signs. A Guggenheim fellowship allowed Bufano to get a sense of puppet theater history in Europe, and with this added perspective, he wrote a number of "how-to" puppet books such as *The Show Book of Remo Bufano* (1929).

Bufano's prolific enthusiasm for and connections to the experiments of the Little Theater Movement led him to break away from the traditional bounds of classic puppet theater to create puppets and masks for Broadway, opera, and other spectacular modes of modern performance. His major early successes in these areas involved the combination of puppets and actors in innovative stage productions. Bufano created puppets and masks for Eva Le Gallienne's popular 1932 production of *Alice in Wonderland* and a show-stopping 35-foot-tall marionette for Billy Rose's 1935 circus musical *Jumbo*—a giant version of the trick marionette clowns of the previous century. Through the League of Composers, an organization devoted to the performance of new music, Bufano entered the realms of high culture, designing and building puppets for two new music works: Manuel de Falla's *El Retablo de Maese Pedro* (*Master Peter's Puppet Show*), and Igor Stravinsky's opera *Oedipus Rex*.

Audiences took notice of the small and life-size marionettes Bufano created in 1924 for de Falla's opera (which was based on an incident in Cervantes's *Don Quixote* involving a puppet performance of the Orlando epic). But his over-life-size marionettes for the 1931 performances of *Oedipus Rex* were a real breakthrough, not simply for puppetry but for modern American theater in general. Bufano's puppets were part of a production created by the United States's most

These three over-life-size puppets, (from left to right, Messenger, Shepherd, Blinded Oedipus) floated above the heads of the chorus in Robert Edmond Jones's production of the Stravinsky opera *Oedipus Rex*. The puppets, made by Remo Bufano, were controlled from below by rods and from above by ropes.

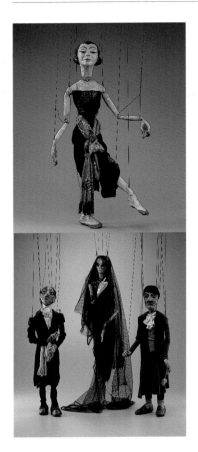

This 1921 portrait puppet of actress Ada Forman (top), made by Lilian Owen Thompson, appeared in the avant-garde revue *Greenwich Village Follies*, which mixed puppet acts with those of live performers.

For a production of Charles Dickens's *Christmas Carol*, Lilian Owen Thompson made the Ghost of the Future out of a new material, cellophane. The ghost stands between Bob Cratchit (left) and Scrooge.

innovative stage designer, Robert Edmond Jones, who had been heavily influenced by Edward Gordon Craig. In a startling new form of opera performance, Bufano's giant puppets, controlled both by ropes from above and rods from below, floated in the air above the heads of the chorus on New York's Metropolitan Opera stage, which was black and devoid of scenery.

As a result of this ground-breaking work, Bufano became New York's most celebrated avant-garde puppeteer, famous for his rough-hewn but inspired productions. His startling success in both the commercial world of Broadway and the high-culture world of opera caused him to believe that a new era of puppet theater was dawning, leading to a 1926 essay for *The Little Review* in which he predicted that America would become the center of a modern puppet renaissance.

Like Sarg, Bufano also used his puppetry skills in the commercial world, designing masks for sale at New York's Bonwit Teller department store, and creating special shows he performed specifically for *Esquire* magazine. For the 1939 World's Fair in New York's Flushing Meadows, Queens, Bufano designed and built ten-foot-tall marionettes for a show in the Hall of Pharmacy, entitled *From Sorcery to Science*. This half-hour spectacle promoting the pharmaceutical

industry was performed continuously on a special revolving stage, whose front was designed to look like a medicine cabinet. The show traced the history of pharmacy from folk remedies to the advent of modern drugstores, and it featured a tape of original music by Aaron Copland, with narration by radio personality Lowell Thomas, an early example of a recorded sound-track providing spoken words and music for a puppet show.

Bufano continued to combine his puppet work with actors' theater, building a woolly mammoth and a dinosaur puppet (the latter of which he performed) for Thornton Wilder's 1944 Broadway production, *The Skin of Our Teeth*. The same year he designed a giant anti-Nazi parading float: a skeleton on horseback playing swastika-decorated drums, for a New York street demonstration sponsored by the Mayor's Committee for Mobilization. Bufano was also interested in the movies and began to explore television puppetry in 1939. His prolific career was cut short when, returning from the West Coast in 1948, he was killed in a plane crash.

While Bufano was clearly the most spectacular figure of the puppet renaissance initiated by the Little Theater Movement, his success was connected to a vibrant community of puppeteers, playwrights, actors, and directors all ready to consider new possibilities

**T**his hand puppet of a bishop was made by Helen Haiman Joseph for a production of *Robin Hood and His Merry Men.*

for puppet theater. For example, the work of Lilian Owen Thompson, a puppeteer who had worked with Maurice Browne in Chicago and then with Tony Sarg in the 1920s, was a welcome addition to the *Greenwich Village Follies*, an annual variety show mixing puppets and live performers. The show began as an avant-garde downtown revue, but proved so popular that it moved to Broadway. Her marionette portraits of contemporary personalities, including actress Ada Forman (for the prologue to the 1921 *Follies*) and the Polish composer Jan Paderewski show how puppets continued to be a consistent element of live commercial entertainment, despite the new high-art contexts in which puppets were often presented. In 1931 Catherine Reighard, an English professor at New York University who used puppets to perform medieval English miracle plays with her students, operated her Puppet Players Studio in Greenwich Village. She performed her own shows and provided space for exhibitions and performances. These included Sarg's and Bufano's innovative work, Agrippino Manteo's Sicilian

Paul McPharlin's 1929 production *Drum Dance* was an experiment in Chinese-style shadow theater, using a script of a traditional Chinese shadow play. Instead of making his shadow figures from leather as the Chinese did, McPharlin built lacquer-painted celluloid puppets. McPharlin's approach to Asian puppet theater was revolutionary, for it respected Chinese culture and did not treat the characters as oddities, as was the practice during the 19th century.

marionettes, and Pauline Benton's Red Gate Shadow Players, who performed traditional Chinese shadow figures.

## PUPPET MODERNISM IN THE MIDWEST

While New York City was a whirling center of commerce, art, and education, the Midwest persisted as a center for making, thinking about, and writing on puppet theater as a modern cultural treasure. A marker of this high-mindedness is the effect of Edward Gordon Craig's romantic idealism on Michael Carmichael Carr, Samuel J. Hume, Ellen Van Volkenburg, Helen Haiman Joseph, and Paul McPharlin, who contributed articles to Craig's journal *The Mask*. But the interest in puppetry as high culture did not at all mean that midwestern puppeteers remained aloof from advertising, publicity, and other forms of commercial life in Chicago,

Detroit, Cleveland, and other cities. Successful professional puppet companies grew and prospered there, and puppeteers consistently found outlets for their work in a variety of commercial contexts. However, the high ideals proposed by Little Theater institutions in the century's second decade continued in the Midwest through the creation of puppet shows as art theater; through work in all levels of the region's educational system and in community theaters focused on puppet theater; and, above all, in McPharlin's dynamic writing, organizing, and theater-making.

Although the Chicago Little Theater's development of modern puppet art theater basically ended with World War I—after which director Ellen Van Volkenburg moved to the West Coast—Helen Haiman Joseph of the Cleveland Playhouse intensified her puppet work from the twenties onward. She started her own professional puppet company in 1925 and created over fourteen different productions for it, ranging from *Robin Hood and His Merry Men* (see p. 65) to *The Life and Death of Doctor Faustus*. According to Paul McPharlin, by 1942 she had nine troupes performing in all parts of the United States. In addition, the resourceful Joseph developed a commercial line of puppets and puppet-building kits for mass distribution (see Appendix).

Paul McPharlin was clearly the most prolific figure in the midwest-

ern puppetry scene; he was active in all areas of its development, and continually built, performed, wrote, and organized for the development of modern puppet performance. Born in Detroit in 1903, McPharlin played with traditional English toy theaters in his youth, and as an undergraduate at Columbia University he studied the international puppet collection amassed by Professor Brander Matthews and took part in puppet productions of French farces directed by a Columbia faculty member, Mathurin Dondo. But his work as a puppeteer began to blossom when he returned to the Midwest after graduation. He formed a "Marionette Fellowship," first in Evanston, Illinois, and then in Detroit, in order to support his puppet shows.

**P**aul McPharlin mixed shadow puppets and rod puppets in his *Noël, or the Mystery of the Nativity* (top). The figures of the angel Gabriel and the three kings are rod puppets, but the image of the camel in the background was made with a shadow puppet.

These two marionettes (right)—Wagner and Bianca—are from Paul McPharlin's production of *Faust*, the story of an alchemist who trades his soul to the devil for knowledge.

From the outset, McPharlin's puppet productions show the range of styles and subject matters typical of modernist puppet art theater. Although his first Marionette Fellowship production was Shakespeare's *Taming of the Shrew* (1928), McPharlin quickly turned to more exotic materials. His 1929 *Drum Dance* was an experiment in Chinese-style shadow theater (see p. 66), using the script of a traditional Chinese shadow play by Tsou Ku Chan Mien, which McPharlin had translated from Berthold Laufer's 1915 collection *Chinesiche Schattenspiele* (*Chinese Shadowplays*). In *Drum Dance*, a prince's jealous wife and his concubine compete for his attention by attempting to dance flawlessly on a set of drums, but the wife turns out to be a witch who uses her magic powers to defeat the

The marionettes of Mozart (above) and his pupil where used by Paul McPharlin for a production of *Mozart in Paris*. McPharlin combined scenes about Mozart with a period ballet and the composer's own 1768 operetta for puppets.

These two marionettes and the piano (left) are from Paul McPharlin's *Pink Plush*, a play about show business in the 1890s.

concubine. Instead of traditional leather puppets, McPharlin built lacquer-painted celluloid puppets and sets that reflected both Chinese design motifs and McPharlin's own sense of modernist minimalism. Some of the advice McPharlin gave on constructing such shadow puppets (in his 1938 edition of Benjamin March's *Chinese Shadow-figure Plays and Their Making*) is an interesting example of practical, inventive modern methods of approaching an ancient puppet tradition. After describing how to construct celluloid shadow figures, McPharlin wrote: "For control sticks umbrella rods are light and strong. They have an eye at one end through which they may be attached with tough cord to holes bored in the hands, necks or feet of the figures. Attach a small battery clip at the end of the rod, rivet leather tabs to the figures where they are to be supported, and catch the tab in the clip for manipulation." It is important to note that McPharlin's approach to Chinese puppet theater was quite novel— even revolutionary—especially in comparison to the nineteenth-century European and American marionette traditions of presenting Chinese characters as clownish circus oddities. McPharlin, benefitting from the increasing volume of new scholarship on Asian theater, took a Chinese play and attempted to do it justice, not by using traditional Chinese shadow puppets, but

by building his own in a manner that at once respected Chinese techniques and styles but also translated them into a modern American idiom.

Also in 1929 McPharlin produced *Noël, or the Mystery of the Nativity*, (see p. 67) medieval-style Christmas play written in 1888 by Maurice Bouchor for Henri Signoret's rod-puppet theater in Paris, an important early example of European puppet art theater. Again, McPharlin translated the text into English, and as in *Drum Dance* he employed a relatively novel puppet technique for the American puppet stage: rod puppets. McPharlin's finely crafted *Noël* rod puppets show his talents as a sculptor and painter. The Three Kings are quite grand figures realized in a stylized modernist aesthetic, but the shepherds and holy family are, as Bouchor suggested in his playscript, realistic figures in contemporary dress, in this case rural midwestern farmers of the 1920s. McPharlin's sculptures succeed as puppets because their effectiveness can only be felt by viewing them from a variety of angles; in other words, they are only fully completed by movement. In addition to using the relatively uncommon technique of rod puppets for *Noël*, McPharlin also used a procession of European-style shadow figures to represent the caravan of animals on which the Three Kings rode. This combination of rod puppets and shadow

Paul McPharlin adapted the characters from George Herriman's celebrated comic strip *Krazy Kat* for a puppet version of *Krazy Kat Ballet*, a "jazz pantomine" written in 1922 by composer John Alden Carpenter. Krazy Kat (top center) stands here between Joe Stork (left) and Bill Postum, who holds a long brush for pasting signs on walls.

These three puppets (below) are from Paul McPharlin's 1936 variety show *Punch's Circus*, which featured both hand and rod puppets. The hand puppet ringmaster (center) would introduce the different acts. Punch (right) is wearing overalls and a hat. (For Punch and Judy, see p. 10.) The motorcycle policeman with his goggles has a modern, almost futuristic look to him.

puppets, like the puppets from *Drum Dance*, marked a real change from the European-style marionettes which had dominated American puppetry. McPharlin was initiating a new sense of world puppet-theater consciousness that would come to dominate western puppet theater as the century progressed.

McPharlin, however, did not at all turn his back on the European puppet traditions, which had until then defined American puppet theater. His version of Hans Christian Andersen's *Chinese Nightingale*, also from 1929, was a familiar European fairy tale performed in a familiar marionette style. This was also the form he used for *Mozart in Paris* (see p. 68), an eighteenth-century variety show and period piece, which McPharlin's Marionette Fellowship performed at the Detroit Institute of Arts in 1934. The production combined marionette scenes, featuring Mozart and a female pupil, with a period ballet, *Les Petits Riens*, and Mozart's 1768 pastoral operetta for puppets, *Bastien and Bastienne*. The latter piece featured the title characters, two shepherds, and Colas, a village magician who brings them together.

Like Remo Bufano's production of *The Little King*, McPharlin's marionette version of *Krazy Kat* (1930) took its inspiration from mass-media, in this case, George Herriman's celebrated comic strip of the same name. Also similar to

that of Bufano, McPharlin's eclectic repertoire grew to include a shadow-figure Purimspiel, in this case written by puppeteer and novelist Meyer Levin in 1932. McPharlin also created a 1934 production of *Dr. Faust* (see p. 67) again using shadow puppets as well as marionettes. He also created "an advertising show for Old English Floor Wax" with hand puppets in 1936, and such oddities as *Lincoln and the Pig*, a comment on the Emancipation Proclamation performed with marionettes by the Detroit Fellowship in 1934, which has surprisingly racist overtones. McPharlin's 1936 *Punch's Circus* was a hand- and rod-puppet variety show featuring such familiar characters as a Ringmaster, and a stereotyped Chinaman, but also an almost futuristically modern goggled Motorcycle Policeman. McPharlin was the State Supervisor of the Michigan Arts and Craft Project of the WPA from 1941 to 1942, and this work was followed by two years of wartime service with the Army Air Force in Mississippi. In addition to designing posters and literature for the troops on the air base, McPharlin also made a "Rookie Joe" marionette for camp show entertainment and safety instruction.

Part of McPharlin's innovative approach to puppet performance was the way he presented his shows. While he took part in the growing demand for school

performances and productions for businesses, McPharlin was also quite concerned with defining puppet theater as relatively high culture. His introduction of puppet classes at Wayne University (now Wayne State University) in Detroit from 1931 to 1938 helped define puppet theater as an intellectually valuable cultural resource. And the Marionette Fellowship itself (as the word "fellowship" suggests) was something more than a simple puppet company. Instead, it reflected McPharlin's desire to combine the integrity and artistry of Old World craft traditions with the mass-production style of modern life so prominent in Detroit. For McPharlin, the puppet productions of the Fellowship were an example of what he once termed "handicraft in the Machine Age"—the possibility that artistic craftsmanship could not only survive in the twentieth century but thrive, despite the omnipresence of manufacturing and machines. This was something McPharlin himself reflected not only in his continuing work in puppet theater but also in his active work in graphic design, typography, and in his designs for shops, storefronts, and manufactured products.

Marjorie Batchelder, McPharlin's friend, partner, and—ultimately—wife, first became interested in puppet theater at the age of twenty-one, when she was asked to paint sets for a marionette production of *Bluebeard* at a summer art camp in

western Massachusetts. Batchelder's involvement only increased, and she pursued puppet theater in the various academic environments central to her later work. Her first performances were in 1931, with students at Florida State College for Women, and her later work grew out of her activites at Ohio State University. This included a marionette production of Aristophanes' *The Birds*, which she created for her Master of Arts degree in 1934. She later formed a company, Marjorie Batchelder's Puppet Players, which performed her puppet productions on tours throughout Ohio and surrounding midwestern states.

Batchelder's 1937 production of Maurice Maeterlinck's *Death of Tintagiles* (see p. 52), besides acknowledging the most prominent European playwright for puppet art theater, shows Batchelder's abiding interest in rod puppets. A relatively novel puppet technique in the United States, rod puppets came to characterize the wide-ranging interests of twentieth-century puppet theater. In a 1936 essay on rod puppets, Batchelder noted their broad cultural history, ranging from Chinese, Javanese, and European traditions to such modern applications as Bufano's giant puppets for *Oedipus Rex*, contemporary parading figures used in urban processions, and McPharlin's *Noël*. The design of Batchelder's wooden rod puppets for *Death of*

*Tintagiles* is closer to Javanese *wayang golek* than to popular European traditions, an interesting indication of the international character modern puppetry was coming to assume. Her continuing connection to puppet art theater led her to produce puppet plays by Edward Gordon Craig and Argentinian puppeteer Javier Villafañe, and her persistent exploration of rod puppetry led to such productions as *Baba Yaga*, created in 1947 for the Columbus Community Theater in Ohio. That was the same year her book *Rod-Puppets and the Human Theater* appeared; it is still considered a central resource on this particular puppet form.

Other midwestern puppeteers included Martin and Olga Stevens of Middlebury, Indiana, who beginning in 1934 developed a repertoire of local and nationwide touring shows that focused primarily on adult audiences. This was unlike most companies, where a desire to reach all ages was tempered by the consistent market demand for children's shows—puppetry having been recognized as an admirable means of entertaining and educating school-age audiences. Although the Stevenses experimented with rod puppets and hand puppets, they focused on marionettes for such shows as *Joan of Arc* (1937) and *Cleopatra* (1940), as well as a *Nativity* and a *Passion Play*, straightforwardly religious plays, which they performed annually beginning in 1935. In their prime the Stevenses Puppets developed into an organization of eight different troupes, and they worked with such puppeteers as Marjorie Batchelder and Rufus Rose. In 1960 the Stevens created a puppet theater correspondence course, which was popular for over two decades.

Martin and Ogla Stevens developed and toured a repertoire of shows intended primarily for adult audiences, including (left to right) *Joan of Arc*, *Cleopatra*, and a *Passion Play*.

Romaine and Ellen Proctor of Springfield, Illinois, started making puppet shows with their children in the 1920s but soon developed their work into a professional company performing children's shows, advertisements, and promotional programs. The Proctor Puppets' repertoire in general avoided the high-art aspirations of McPharlin and Batchelder, but the Proctors found regular and consistent audiences for their work. They converted a Springfield movie house into a puppet theater in 1935, and their regular touring schedule included health education shows at state fairs in Iowa, Illinois, and Indiana. The backdrops and marionettes for *Jack and the Beanstalk* offer an indication of what a typical touring show of the period looked like, with straightforward, colorful props and puppets telling an enthralling fairy tale.

## MODERN PUPPETRY ON THE WEST COAST

In San Francisco, Perry Dilley began playing with hand puppets in 1919 and continued to concentrate on this puppet form throughout his career. Early shows at California universities, theaters, and clubs included plays from nineteenth-century Parisian hand puppeteer Émile Duranty, as well as Nikolai Evreinov's *A Merry Death*, a Russian Symbolist play with *commedia dell'arte* characters. By 1924 Ellen Van Volkenburg had

**T**he marionette of Oberon (above), king of the fairies, was made by Perry Dilley for a West Coast production of *A Midsummer Night's Dream*.

Romaine and Ellen Proctor's *Jack and the Beanstalk* (opposite, top) was typical of touring shows of the 1930s and '40s. The giant is at the far right; Jack and his mother stand near the cow. The mother is a self-portrait of Ellen Proctor, who served as curator of the McPharlin Collection from 1970 to 1982.

Perry Dilley's backdrops for his production of *The Tinker and the Teakettle* (opposite, bottom) were influenced by modernist design.

moved to the West Coast, and Dilley built new marionettes for her revival of *A Midsummer Night's Dream*; the following year he went to Ohio to direct puppet productions at the Cleveland Playhouse. Dilley returned to the West Coast and performed at theaters and colleges in the San Francisco Bay area, continuing to focus on classic plays from the European puppet repertoire by such writers as Lemercier de Neuville and Maurice Sand. In the 1930s Dilley made a hand-puppet show from a Japanese fable, *The Tinker and the Teakettle*. The choice of Asian literature as a basis for a puppet show was part of the developing international sense of puppet theater, but this traditional subject contrasted with the modernist designs Dilley used for his backdrops. A forest of trees is contrived of almost abstract geometric shapes, and Dilley's perspective interiors of the Japanese buildings look like Frank Lloyd Wright designs. Dilley's puppets are colorful and exotic Asians, but, like McPharlin's *Drum Dance* figures, they are presented as characters, not caricatures.

Not far from Perry Dilley's San Francisco studio was an old warehouse, which puppeteer Blanding Sloan converted into a puppet theater in 1928. It was here that Sloan, who had previously worked with Michael Carmichael Carr and Remo Bufano, persuaded Ralph Chessé to produce his early marionette shows. Chessé had started out as an actor and a painter from New Orleans and had worked in New York at the Neighborhood Playhouse. His puppet work in San Francisco clearly paralleled the lofty goals of puppet art theater in the East and Midwest: to present, as Paul McPharlin put it, "adult productions of drama comparable to those of the human theater." Chessé's 1928 production of Shakespeare's *Macbeth*, in Sloan's theater, showed his confidence in puppet theater's ability to approach the highest reaches of English-language drama, but his marionette version of Eugene O'Neill's *Emperor Jones* of that year marks an even more important shift for modern American puppet theater.

O'Neill's play was first performed in 1920 by actors at the Provincetown Playhouse (perhaps including Remo Bufano) in a production that already incorporated life-size puppets and objects. *The Emperor Jones* focuses on an African-American fugitive, Brutus Jones, who flees the United States to live out a kind of megalomaniacal fantasy as "emperor" of a Caribbean island suggestive of Haiti. When the natives rise against him, Jones flees into the jungle, and in a series of encounters confronts scenes not only from his personal past but from the collective experience of blacks since the advent of the slave trade. O'Neill's play was a startling innovation because it combined Freudian con-

Ralph Chessé's marionette version of Eugene O'Neill's *Emperor Jones* marked an important shift for modern American puppet theater in its attempt to deal with issues of race and ethnicity. The title character, Brutus Jones (opposite), illustrates Chessé's skill at sculpting strong, stark characters, filled with a certain gravity and dignity. The marionette is a portrait of the actor Charles Gilpin, who appeared as Jones in the Federal Theater Project's production of the play.

cepts only then seeping into public consciousness; a dramatic structure indebted to German expressionist theater; and a brave attempt to deal with race as a pivotal American problem. Ralph Chessé's production of the play marks a similarly bold attempt to transform American puppet theater, whose attention to race and ethnicity had previously been limited to the minstrel stereotypes of black characters depicted in Punch and Judy shows and nineteenth-century marionette variety spectacles. Chessé's sculptures of Jones, his pursuers, and the dissolute white colonialist Smithers all show strong, stark character and expression, and a certain gravity and emotion quite missing from Daniel Meader's disturbingly happy minstrels of the late 1800s. Neither O'Neill's play nor Chessé's marionette production completely succeeded in avoiding some ethnic stereotyping (perhaps inevitable in forms which depend on a kind of visual shorthand for their strength), but, like McPharlin's production of *Drum Dance*, they mark an effort by puppeteers of European heritage to seriously consider other races and cultures.

Chessé followed his production of *The Emperor Jones* with classics by Shakespeare and Molière, as well as *Uncle Tom's Cabin*, Gilbert and Sullivan's *Mikado*, and *Dr. Jekyll and Mr. Hyde*, among others. In the 1950s, Cheesé taught puppetry at the college level and was among

Eugene O'Neill's play *The Emperor Jones* was loosely based on the life of Henri Christophe, a leader in Haiti's independence movement who proclaimed himself king of the island in 1907. In the scene below, the Jones character sits on his throne, flanked by one of his subjects and another island resident, a dissolute white colonialist.

the early puppeteers to venture into television with his 1951 marionette series *Brother Buzz*, which stayed on the air for fourteen years. But throughout his career he was consistent in his pursuit of puppet modernism. "A good puppeteer," he said in the 1980s, "must study theater in all its phases and read Gordon Craig."

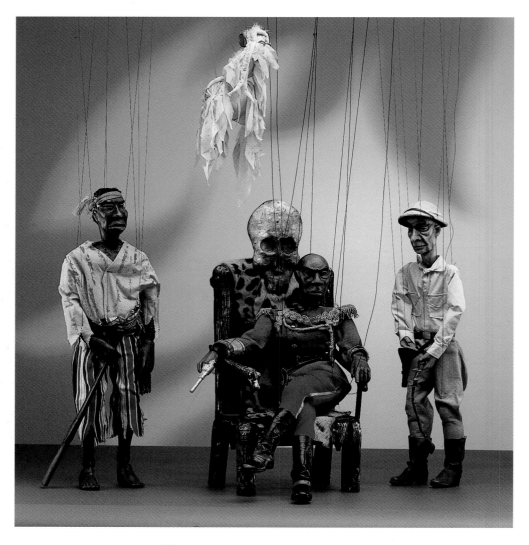

## THE FIRST PUPPETRY CONFERENCE

The puppet revival of the early twentieth century reached a particular plateau with the first American Puppetry Conference and Festival, held in Detroit in the summer of 1936. Paul McPharlin, unsurprisingly, was at the center of this activity. He organized the event himself, creating a culminating moment in American puppet modernism, where a sense of the increased expectations and possibilities for puppet theater in an array of contemporary cultural contexts was matched by a wide-ranging understanding of puppet traditions around the world. The two exhibitions at the conference give a sense of the new outlook achieved by two decades of puppet modernism. One exhibit featured an array of puppets from Europe and Asia, including Chinese shadow figures, Javanese *wayang golek* and *wayang kulit* puppets, Japanese hand puppets, Sicilian marionettes, Catalan hand puppets, a poster from Nina Efimova's Russian puppet theater, and hand puppets by Max Jacob, who was part of the European art-puppet movement. The other exhibit featured contemporary work by American puppeteers, including Sarg, Bufano, Batchelder, Chessé, Dilley, McPharlin, the Proctors, Rufus Rose, Martin Stevens, and W. A. Dwiggins.

Performances at the conference also show the wider scope of puppet modernism. They included a Petrushka show; Shakespeare's *Taming of the Shrew* by the Tatterman Marionettes; a *Passion Play* "reverently offered" by the Martin Marionettes of Cincinnati; McPharlin's version of *Doctor Faust*, based on a nineteenth-century German marionette script; Marjorie Batchelder's *Saint George and the Dragon*; and the "world première" of an autobiographical puppet play especially written by Gertrude Stein for Chicago puppeteer Don Vestal: *Identity, or, I Am because My Little Dog Knows Me*.

This sense of the variety of worldwide puppet forms and the innovative possibilities they offered contemporary puppeteers was reinforced by the talks presented at the conference. George Middleton delivered an address about his life as a member of his family's nineteenth-century English marionette troupe, and Marjorie Batchelder gave a wide-ranging lecture about rod-puppet theater, touching on Chinese and Javanese traditions, Henri Signoret's Parisian innovations, the Manteo family's Sicilian puppets, Bufano's *Oedipus Rex*, and her own rod-puppet experiments. Tony Sarg gave a talk explaining how he had become the United States's most recognized puppeteer; Rufus Rose gave a how-to lecture on marionette technique; and a series of different

speakers analyzed the possibilities of puppetry for library storytelling, art education, occupational therapy, and as a way through which mothers could inspire "the necessary make-believe world of play" in their children.

The idea of a conference and festival of puppet theater was itself novel. Before the advent of modern puppetry, such puppeteers as George Middleton's parents and grandparents were for the most part unschooled, working-class performers trying to survive by presenting whatever type of entertainment might attract a paying audience. To hold a conference about the artistic, educational, and commercial possibilities of the form would probably have appeared to them as unusual as the idea that non-western forms of puppet theater might be worth studying and understanding. But by 1936, the time was right for an event that could absorb the classicism of *wayang kulit* together with the high modernism of Gertrude Stein, and so suggest the possibility of new projects achievable by a nationwide community of puppeteers. In particular, discussions at the Detroit conference led to the founding of the Puppeteers of America the following year, a group that has continued into the twenty-first century as the central organizational focus of American puppeteers. ◆

This delightful puppet portrait of Greta Garbo on, of all things, roller skates was part of a nightclub variety show performed by the Lauer Sisters. Other parts of their act included a tap dancer, a ballerina, and a marionette seal.

If the first wave of puppet modernism began in 1915 at the Chicago Little Theater, it reached a certain culmination with Paul McPharlin's American Puppetry Conference of 1936. The conference, full of hope and new spirits even in the midst of the Depression, defined a wide range of opportunities for puppet

theater, most of which were in fact pursued by American puppeteers in the decades to come. ◆ If the first wave flowered in the fertile range of possibilities suggested by the 1936 conference, a second wave of puppet modernism can be said to have grown with the Depression-era boost given puppetry by the Federal Theater Project, part of the

Works Progress Administration (WPA), from 1935 to 1939. This growth was consolidated—or institutionalized—by the creation of the Puppeteers of America in 1937. The second wave built on the first wave's sense of puppetry as a serious art form for audiences of all ages, a goal which was reinforced by the ideals of Federal Theater Project puppet productions. However, the second wave developed in different directions than the first. The hallmarks of this second revival became an increased identification of puppet theater as performance to entertain and to teach children; a continuing popularity as adult theater, although more in the context of nightclub entertainment than dramatic plays; an increased awareness of the possibilities of puppet theater for publicity and advertising; and the development of new forms of puppet theater in the emerging medium of television.

During the 1930s, the marionette units of the Federal Theater Project (FTP) were not simply a means of keeping puppeteers employed but a nationwide endorsement of puppet theater as an important artistic and social medium capable of entertaining and educating audiences of all ages and backgrounds at a particularly difficult moment in United States history. In other words, the FTP marionette units echoed many of the goals of early puppet modernism but on a national, government-supported level. Federally funded puppet groups included the marionette units lead by Remo Bufano, Ralph Chessé, David Lano, and other puppeteers, and the Michigan Arts and Craft Project led by McPharlin. These groups not only employed hundreds of puppeteers around the country but also presented an average of one hundred shows per week. The repertoire featured children's classics and variety shows, as well as productions for adults like a remounted version of Chessé's 1928 *Emperor Jones*. It was in this environment that Bil Baird's hand puppets appeared as high art, performing the Seven Deadly Sins in Orson Welles's acclaimed FTP production of *Doctor Faustus* in New York. But marionette units could also play more humble roles; one unit, for example, toured throughout the eastern United States an educational show about careless driving.

As head of the New York marionette unit of the Federal Theater Project, Bufano supervised scores of puppet builders, writers, and performers in the production of forty-seven different puppet shows (including *Oliver Twist*, *Sherlock Holmes*, and even *Kuan Kung's Generosity*, a marionette version of a classic Chinese epic). Over a thousand different performances of such shows were held, making the marionette group the most successful New York unit of the FTP. However, Bufano quit the organization in 1937, protesting "obstructive policies" that prevented him, he charged, from mounting a production of Czech playwright Karel Yapek's *R.U.R.*, a controversial melodrama about rebellious robots and the dangers of technology (the term "robot," in fact, emerged from the play).

Chessé served as the California state director of the Federal Theater

Project puppetry division and was inspired by the range of puppet activities over which he presided during that time. He felt that the FTP gave American puppet theater a tremendous boost by supporting the development of puppet shows for adults (a central goal of puppet modernism). He wrote:

> Federal Theater gave me a chance to show that marionettes can be very high-class adult entertainment. We could go into the classics, which is something others hadn't done; they were still doing the fairy tales for children....The variety shows I did were adult productions. The Federal Theater was sponsoring a whole new program in theater, and marionettes had to get out of the rut.

If the Federal Theater Project marked the nation's sense of the value of puppet theater, the 1936 Puppet Conference marked the desire of American puppeteers to continue to develop their theater as a multivalanced art form able to entertain, teach, and persuade audiences across the United States. However, while the various educational, social, and therapeutic goals outlined at the 1936 conference were pursued in the ensuing decades, the particular circumstances of the mid-twentieth century shifted the relative importance of these goals. While a sense of the

These two "Spanish dancers" were part of the Lauer Sisters' nightclub act.

---

**CONVERSATION BETWEEN TWO PUPPETS**

Puppet 1: "What if something should happen to us?"
Puppet 2: "What do you mean?"

Puppet 1: "So we couldn't act any more. If there wouldn't be any more puppeteers who knew how to work us?"
Puppet 2: "They'd put us in a museum maybe. How lonesome it will be, buried in a glass case!"
Puppet 1: "That's all right. Perhaps we'll be put in with some nice African masks!"

Both (leaning toward audience): "Please, if any of you ever sees us there in the museum, just nod to us. That will be a sign that you saw us in the better days, and that we found a place not only in the museum, but in your hearts."

---

"Pensive Puppets," by Nina Efimova, translated by Elena Mitcoff. From *Puppet Plays*, Paul McPharlin, ed., 1937.

These three self-portraits of the Lauer Sisters show them in elegant evening gowns. But, in a move that reiterated 19th-century racial stereotypes, they turned themselves into African-American "mammies" by placing a black-faced puppet mask over each of the three heads.

educational role of puppet theater remained consistent, the idea of puppet theater as a "serious" adult form of performance—an arena, for example where plays by Shakespeare, O'Neill, and Gertrude Stein or an opera by Stravinsky might be performed—became less important as the desire for and necessity of economic survival tended to make entertainment a more pressing goal than "artistic" puppet theater. The traditional function of puppets as entertainers led puppeteers to play a prominent role in nightclub variety acts; the persuasive powers of puppetry were increasingly used to represent corporations and to sell commercial products; and the pressing demands of the marketplace often lead puppeteers to create shows expressly geared for children. Perhaps most importantly, the newly evolving medium of television could fully use all three of these aspects of puppet theater.

This is not to say that puppetry ceased to fulfill its traditional social roles, because puppets remained central to modern articulations of public political performance in the United States. For centuries in Europe Punch, Kasperl, Petrushka, and other local archetypes had acted as political gadflies, critiquing local authorities with an air of rebelliousness. Such impulses persisted in the twentieth century, although, as in the case of the Red Petrushka puppets, social and political criticism could be subject

to stronghanded regulation by national authorities. In the United States, especially from the 1920s to the '40s, puppets were used in intriguing political contexts. In 1936 painter Jackson Pollock and other young artists learned from Mexican muralist David Siquieros how to make giant parading figures for May Day demonstrations in New York's Union Square. By the time Remo Bufano made his design for a giant anti-Nazi parade float during World War II, an American tradition of puppet performance in political demonstrations had developed, from Union Square to the factories of Detroit, where striking auto workers used homemade dummies, signs, and other visually arresting objects to call attention to their cause. During and immediately after World War II, puppeteers like Paul McPharlin (with his wartime marionette Rookie Joe) and Alfred Wallace (with his hand-puppet caricatures) carried on the tradition of politically persuasive puppet theater. The Cold War climate of the late 1940s and '50s dampened such expressions until their revival during the social upheavals of the 1960s.

## NIGHTCLUBS AND VARIETY THEATER

An area of American puppetry that became increasingly popular in the 1930s and '40s was performances in cabaret and nightclub shows.

Ventriloquists had been active in vaudeville theater since the late nineteenth century and were now equally popular in nightclubs and cabarets. In the 1930s they were joined by puppeteers, elegantly dressed in tuxedos or evening gowns, who worked their puppets—usually marionettes—in full view of the audience, without a puppet stage. As in ventriloquism, the success of the puppet performance relied on the persuasive illusion of a living puppet despite the obvious presence of its operator. On the one hand these particularly American forms of nightclub puppetry were part of the persistent vitality and flexibility of European-style variety-show performance; but on the other they also marked an unintended congruence with Asian puppet forms like Bunraku, whose puppeteers are also always in full view of the audience, without any diminution of the puppets' dramatic power.

These cabaret and nightclub puppet acts included Herb Scheffel, a New York puppeteer who in the 1930s and '40s used hand puppets, marionettes, and finger puppets for short skits in circuses and variety-show revues, which he performed in such unusual venues as Schrafft's Restaurant in midtown Manhattan. His "Bubbles Divine" finger puppet is a typical cabaret character: glamorous and sexy.

The Lauer Sisters were another such act, and their marionettes

Alfred Wallace jumped into the world of politics with his puppet performances. He depicted a U.S. senator literally as a two-faced politican, who could be turned around to show his other side (as shown below). Among Wallace's politically oriented puppets included (opposite, clockwise from upper left) President Franklin D. Roosevelt as Punch's baby; a Tired World, which turns into a flat world when its handle is squeezed; a portrait of U.S. labor leader John L. Lewis, and French leader Charles de Gaulle.

reflect the quirky variety of such performance: a marionette seal, a ballerina, a tap dancer, a music professor and a piano, two "Spanish Dancers" (see p. 83), and a delightfully unlikely portrait puppet of movie star Greta Garbo on roller skates (see p. 80). A more bizarre act presented the three Lauer Sisters themselves in the form of transformation puppets: first as smiling, pink-skinned beauties in identical black floor-length gowns, holding green scarves, and then, through the addition of puppet masks, as grinning African-American mammies, complete with red-and-white checkered head scarves. While perhaps not as blatant as nineteenth-century minstrel stereotypes, which had become dated with the demise of actual minstrel shows, these three marionettes indicate that issues of race and identity still could not be seriously addressed in the realm of popular entertainment. That left the art-theaters, with productions of such fare as O'Neill's expressionistic *Emperor Jones*, to try to focus on race in a meaningful and thought-provoking way.

Another active member of New York's puppet community was Alfred Wallace, who started creating puppet shows with children in the 1930s as part of a crafts program at a community center. He began to perform with hand puppets and rod puppets in musical revues in the late 1930s and soon put together a nightclub act called *Alfred Wallace and His Dancing Puppets*. During World War II, he played his *Show Within a Show* over 1,600 times for American soldiers in Europe. In the postwar years, he performed such pieces as *Goober is My Name* and *Johnny Gremlin Varieties* across the United States, and made television commercials. Wallace did not hesitate to jump into the tricky field of politics but did so with a great sense of humor. Wallace used puppets to turn President Franklin D. Roosevelt into Punch's baby, with a long yellow dress, and to depict a U.S. senator quite literally as a two-faced politician—a canny use of puppetry's special sculptural possibilities. The concerned, questioning frown of his "Tired World" rod puppet of 1950 is a similarly clever evocation of postwar fears at the beginning of the Cold War. The same set of puppets included a

Frank Paris was a highly successful cabaret performer prior to his
becoming one of the first puppeeters
to appear on television. His *Stars on
Strings* featured marionette portraits
of well-known peronalities such as
singer-dancer Josephine Baker and
Olympic figure skater and movie
actress Sonia Henie.

panoply of international figures depicted as hand puppets, including French leader Charles de Gaulle, U.S. labor leader John L. Lewis, Joseph Stalin (as a Russian bear), and Uncle Sam.

Perhaps the most successful American nightclub puppeteer was Frank Paris, who started building a variety puppet show in 1928 after reading an article about Tony Sarg. Paris's popularity as a cabaret performer led him to tour across the country in the late 1930s with *Stars on Strings*, a variety show featuring such marionette portrait characters as Olympic skater Sonja Henie (on skates, of course) and the flamboyant singer-dancer Josephine Baker (see p. 88). These figures counted on audience familiarity with the original stars, and a successful performance played on canny similarities and stark contrasts between human and puppet. Other characters in Paris's variety acts included an ostrich ballerina in toe shoes and a feminine skeleton in red high-heel shoes, gloves, and hat. The latter could perform the tried-and-true marionette transformation trick of separating its bones into independent dancing objects and reuniting them back into a complete figure, just as Walter Deaves had done in the late nineteenth century (see p. 28).

American nightclub puppeteers might seem to have been concerned only with providing benign entertainment to fun-loving audiences,

but the nature of puppets as enigmatic performers of essential symbols was inevitably connected to something like Paris's dancing skeleton and its grandly entertaining dance of death, just as the Lauer Sisters' black mammy figures reiterated stereotypes of race, which for decades had been central to the background of American culture.

## TOWARDS FILM AND TELEVISION

As early as 1939, puppeteers began to investigate the possibilities of the new medium of television. Remo Bufano first began his exploration of television puppetry in that year, but in the late 1940s these experiments intensified when he worked in Los Angeles on various film and television projects combining marionettes and stop-action puppet animation. Burr Tillstrom first tried his hand at television puppetry in 1939, although it was not until 1947 that he was offered his own show, which later became the well-known *Kukla, Fran, and Ollie* program. In fact, it was Frank Paris's shift to television performance in the late 1940s that first seemed to mark the wave of the future.

In 1947 Paris produced *The Adventures of Toby* as a weekly marionette soap opera for NBC television. This led to an invitation from NBC the same year for Paris to build puppets for *Puppet Playhouse*,

Before his successful foray into television puppetry, Burr Tillstrom created puppets for industrial shows. This marionette, with a lightning bolt emblazoned on his cap, was used in the making of a short film for General Electric.

The name Kukla comes from the Russian word for puppet—*kukl*—suggested to Tillstrom by a Russian ballerina whose marionette portrait he made in 1939.

a program that eventually became the extremely popular *Howdy Doody Show*. The following year, Paris demanded merchandising rights for the Howdy Doody puppet he had built for the show. NBC refused, and Paris left the network, taking his marionette with him. Forbidden to use the name Howdy Doody, Paris renamed his puppet Peter Pixie, and performed it on a New York City children's show, but this project did not achieve the success of the puppet's original incarnation.

Although Paris was one of the first puppeteers to appear on television, other puppeteers proved to be far more successful in the new medium. As a child, Burr Tillstrom of Chicago was encouraged to pursue puppetry by one of Tony Sarg's sisters, who lived across the street from him. At the age of nineteen Tillstrom had been a puppeteer in Don Vestal's 1936 production of Gertrude Stein's *Identity* at the Detroit Puppetry Conference; but he soon began to perform his own shows in Chicago city parks, as part of a program connected to the WPA. In 1939 he was invited to present weekly shows at Marshall Field's department store, which led to the establishment of a permanent puppet theater in the store. Tillstrom created scores of productions for Marshall Field's, many of which incorporated toy hand puppets available for purchase in the toy department. He also made

marionettes for industrial shows sponsored by such companies as General Electric.

Tillstrom worked with television as early as 1939 and quickly decided that the new medium would be the best outlet for his puppet shows. In 1947 a Chicago television station, WBKB, offered him a regular hour-long program, *Junior Jamboree*, for which he operated hand puppets. He invited Fran Allison, a Chicago radio personality, to act as narrator and foil. Tillstrom's hand puppets—Kukla, the bucktoothed dragon, and Ollie, the wry, bald-headed human—were the central characters in a growing population of puppet personalities, the "Kuklapolitans," who soon gained nationwide popularity.

The show moved to NBC's Chicago affiliate in 1949, where it was retitled *Kukla, Fran, and Ollie*, and later went on to be broadcast on the NBC network. By 1952, according to the *Puppetry Journal*, 5.5 million television sets were tuned to the show five nights a week; the Kuklapolitan Players had won "sixteen major awards for showmanship excellence," and Tillstrom's show had, at least in the United States, become synonymous with the word puppetry. Tillstrom and Allison sustained their immense popularity for eight more years. They improvised all their shows in the studio, never relying on written scripts, and resisted the sponsors' efforts to influence the content of their work. Tillstrom operated his hand puppets behind a translucent cloth screen, watching a video monitor to gauge his movements according to the frame of the television camera.

Tillstrom was an early initiator of what would become the most popular twentieth-century medium for puppets—a choice that made him wealthy—but he also had a sense of puppet theater consistent with the wider goals of the puppet art movement he had known since

Burr Tillstrom, best known for his long-running television show *Kukla, Fran, and Ollie*, turned to less commercial fare with his marionette adaptation of L. Frank Baum's *Land of Oz*. The second title in Baum's popular series of Oz books, *Land of Oz* featured some of the same characters as the better-known *Wonderful Wizard of Oz*, like the Tin Woodsman (below, far right), while introducing such new ones as Jack Pumkinhead (center). Tillstrom's production was filmed for broadcast on television (right).

the 1930s. In 1950 he commented that although puppet theater in other societies had historically functioned as a central cultural activity for all ages, "for some reason, people in this country have always been kind of haughty about puppets. They seem to think that they're only for kids." Tillstrom wanted to widen the range of his work (although *Kukla, Fran, and Ollie* appealed to adults as well as children) and to create his own puppet theater as well as a school of puppetry. In 1950, in fact, he did momentarily turn away from his popular television work to produce a little-known marionette adaptation of L. Frank Baum's *Land of Oz*, the second in Baum's popular series of Oz books. Tillstrom's version, featuring colorful versions of Baum's fanciful

characters, was intended for broadcast, but after a pilot film was made, the project was abandoned.

George Latshaw, a Cleveland puppeteer who worked with Martin and Olga Stevens and Burr Tillstrom in the late 1940s, began to make his own puppet shows in the 1950s. His marionette version of Manuel de Falla's classic *El Retablo de Maese Pedro* was produced for the Cleveland Music School Settlement in 1955, and Latshaw followed this production the same year with hand-puppet versions of *Jack and the Beanstalk* and *Rumpelstiltskin*. Latshaw taught and performed puppetry in local schools, but like many puppeteers he also found work in mass media. He operated one of the "Carrot Top" hand puppets

for the 1953 film *Lili* (about the romance between a French village girl and a worldly puppeteer) and produced a series of different puppet shows for Cleveland television stations.

Latshaw's work shows a fascination with many different forms of puppet theater, and his 1961 version of *The Pied Piper* introduced Latshaw's innovative "flippet" puppets: flat cutout hand puppet figures of cardboard or plywood based on simple geometric forms and painted in bright primary colors, whose features could change according to Latshaw's adept manipulation. Manipulating the flippet puppets, Latshaw wrote, was "like balancing a croquet ball on two fingers, while trying to use chop sticks with the other three." At the instigation of the Detroit Institute of Arts, Latshaw produced a number of shows with the Detroit Symphony Orchestra. These included the American première of Debussy's *La Boite à Joujoux* (*The Jewelry Box*), which Latshaw mounted with rod puppets, and his version of Aaron Copland's ballet *Billy the Kid*, for which Latshaw used colorful over-life-size rod puppets visibly operated (in the manner of Bunraku figures

Geeorge Latshaw called these flat, cutout hand puppets flippets. A puppet's features could change according to Latshaw's adept manipulation of the figure.

or Bufano's *Oedipus Rex*) by puppeteers dressed in black.

Rufus and Margo Rose were once billed as "America's foremost artists of the Marionette Theater," and their work spanned five decades, from the 1930s to the 1970s. They met while working with Tony Sarg's puppet company in 1928, married in 1931, and soon began their own puppet company, which performed such productions as *Dick Whittington and His Cat*, *Hansel and Gretel*, and *Ali Baba and the Forty Thieves* on coast-to-coast tours through the 1930s. Like many successful puppeteers of the period, the Roses worked in a variety of different forms and venues, performing for the A&P Company at the 1933 World's Fair in Chicago, and making the first commercial film using marionettes—*Jerry Pulls the Strings*—for the American Can Company in 1938. Like Burr Tillstrom, the Roses were drawn to the new medium of television, most famously following Frank Paris by performing in the long-running *Howdy Doody* show during the 1950s. In 1942 the Roses built a permanent theater and studio in Waterford, Connecticut, which attracted local audiences to their marionette performances and also hosted numerous Puppeteers of America festivals. Margo Rose designed many of their marionettes, and Rufus constructed the puppets and their controls, coming up with

new ways to cast molded puppet heads and new methods of marionette string controls. The Roses worked with a variety of different puppeteers, teaching manipulation techniques to Burr Tillstrom and Jim Henson, among others.

The use of puppets for advertising and commercial purposes was another major development in American puppetry in the last half of the twentieth century, often tied to the increasing number of television programs for children. The idea of using puppets for advertising and in commercial productions predates the popularity of the new medium of television. In 1933 Tony Sarg's puppets appeared in a supermarket chain's display at the Chicago World's Fair. Remo Bufano, Burr Tillstrom, and numerous others provided puppets for a variety of commercial exhibitions at the 1939 New York World's Fair, and Tillstrom used his puppet shows at Chicago's Marshall Field's department store to boost retail sales of hand puppets. But a sense of conflict between the world of advertising and commercial entertainment and the vision of puppet theater as an independent art was consistently a point of debate among American puppeteers.

When Paul McPharlin viewed the scores of puppet shows at the 1939 World's Fair in New York City, he was impressed by their high quality, which, he wrote "set a new standard for artistic and

**T**his private eye puppet was made by Rufus and Margo Rose, who where once billed as the country's "foremost artists of the Marionette theater." Margo Rose designed many of their marionettes, while Rufus Rose constructed them and made the controllers.

J ero Magon saw his puppet work as part of the expressionist art movement of the early twentieth century, which embraced the idea of depicting an artist's inner vision. In this self-portrait hand puppet, he has dressed himself as a painter in a smock and beret.

technical excellence." However, McPharlin was surprised at the extent to which commercialism pervaded the performances, and asked "what did they have to say as puppets? 'Buy Jell-o' and 'Use Lucite'! And they were not, in all the shows, even entertaining saying it." Interestingly, McPharlin did not place responsibility for this situation on the puppeteers themselves but on "the advertisers they worked for." In McPharlin's opinion, American advertisers had simply been more attuned to the possibilities of puppet theater than the general public, which, in his opinion, had "never supported puppets so handsomely as the advertisers did at this fair." And puppeteers, he added, "are quick to know which side their bread is buttered on."

Lou Bunin, a New York-based puppeteer who produced Eugene O'Neill's *Hairy Ape* with puppets in 1929, made an animated film for the Petroleum Building at the 1939 World's Fair and produced a stop-motion version of *Alice in Wonderland* with puppets and actors in the late 1940s. He was, by 1952, also critical of the commercial influence on puppet shows—this time in the burgeoning medium of television. "In the United States," he wrote in a *Puppetry Journal* essay, "television, like radio, is primarily an advertising media." And in addition to the forces of science and art, Bunin felt, there was a "Powerful Third Force" ("PTF") which controlled the airwaves:

the sponsor. Bunin felt that successful television puppet shows were "not just puppet shows," but "super-hucksters on a national scale....The sheer mountain of consumer's goods sold by Howdy Doody," Bunin wrote, "makes the great PTF jiggle with joy."

This concern was also shared by some television puppeteers themselves, like Bob Keeshan, who played the role of Captain Kangaroo on CBS in a show sponsored by Wonder Bread, Kellogg Cereals, and Schwinn Bicycles, with commercials often narrated by Keeshan. *Captain Kangaroo*, according to Keeshan, actually operated at a loss, costing CBS $1 million a year; but Keeshan felt there should be more shows with "entertainment and educational value" for children. The television networks and their sponsors, Keeshan said, "could easily absorb the kind of costs without feeling the pinch on their pocket books. But they are narrow. If sponsors can't sell a car or toothpaste right now, they don't want to make an investment in the future."

Clearly a major element of the second wave of puppet modernism was its adaptability to the particular situation of postwar American consumer culture and, in particular, the rise of new media like television, whose massive audiences and powerful commercial content made the art-theater aspirations of the 1936 Puppet Conference seem almost quaint. But the vision of an

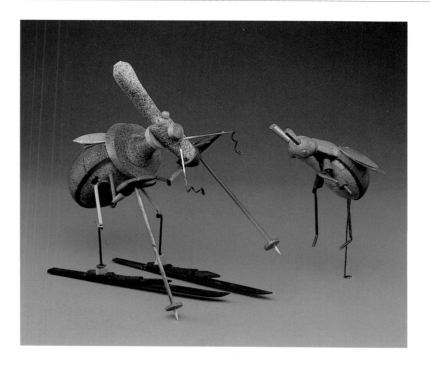

**B**asil Milovsoroff took his inspiration from the materials he used in making his whimsical, non-realistic puppets. The skiing bug (left), a rod puppet, is carved out of wood with metal legs.

artistic puppet theater devoted to innovative live performances did not disappear; instead it developed in mid-century through the work of puppeteers like Jero Magon and Basil Milovsoroff.

Jero Magon began his own pursuit of puppet modernism in New York with a 1933 production of *The Emperor Jones*, using marionettes and flat rod puppets. He followed this with a production of another O'Neill play, *Marco Millions*, at Carnegie Hall's Chamber Music Hall in 1938; this time he used marionettes and shadow figures. Magon considered his puppet work part of the expressionist art movement of the early twentieth century, in which

"art becomes a revelation" of the artist's "inner vision, expressed in images that have a life of their own."

Born in Siberia in 1907, Basil Milovsoroff immigrated to the United States at the age of twenty and by the 1930s had defined himself as a puppeteer. Based in rural Vermont from the 1930s through the 1950s, he created a variety of puppet shows based on Russian folktales, as well as making public service films. He then spent fifteen years as a professor of Russian at Dartmouth College, returning to full-time puppet theater after retiring from teaching. Milovsoroff insistently designed non-realistic puppets, taking his inspiration directly from the materials he used

and assembling different objects and materials—gnarled roots were his trademark—into abstract "machines" and whimsical characters. In 1951 Milovsoroff wrote that "the Puppet Theater offers us the near-ultimate in theater make-believe." His persistent belief in the power of abstract spectacle and more importantly in puppetry as, above all, an art theater, was consistent with the idealistic goals of visionaries like Gordon Craig. But just as Magon's 1930s conception of puppet theater as high art became a rarer vision in the 1930s and '40s, by the 1950s Milovsoroff's similar goals seemed, oddly enough, almost out of place. ◆

This early version of Kermit the Frog, perhaps the best known of the Muppet characters, is not a functioning puppet. He has been permanently mounted in this pose, perhaps to be more easily photographed, and can no longer move. Jim Henson and Jane Nebel first created Muppets, hybrid hand and rod puppets, in the late 1950s.

During the first half of the twentieth century, two successive waves of puppet

modernism helped define an array of different forms and functions of American

puppet theater. At the outset of the century, the first wave declared that puppet

theater could create high art as well as popular entertainment, that it could

equal actors' theater in 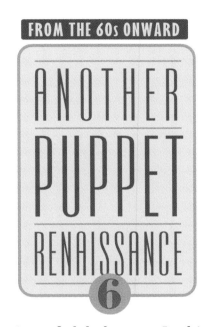 its capacity to inspire

adult audiences, and that it could excel as

a provider of cultural nourishment for

children. As the century settled into the seri-

ously modern challenges of the Depression, then

World War II, and the Cold War that followed,

American puppet theater developed its survival

skills by perfecting its functionality in an

increasingly technological society of global scope. In this second wave, puppeteers

proved themselves amazingly adept in utilizing the possibilities of television and

film and in creating solid work for themselves in children's theater and advertising.

In other words, by the end of the 1950s, American puppet theater had estab-

lished itself in a network of related niches: live variety shows, department store

performances, school and community center programs, church performances, and above all television, where the most exposure and financial awards lay. Similar trends marked the concurrent development of puppet theater in Europe, on both sides of the Cold War's Iron Curtain. In addition, European governments—especially the socialist and Communist ones—had followed the sense of theater as cultural treasure by supporting scores of permanent puppet theaters employing full-time performers, technicians, writers, and administrators to create and present new and traditional shows. Such situations, of course, did not exist in the United States, except for the Depression era, when federal programs supported puppeteers and puppetry across the country.

Although the creation of a puppet art theater for adult audiences—puppetry as a legitimate form of modern culture—had been one of the dreams of the Little Theater Movement in the 1910s, the goal seemed distant or impossible by the second half of the century. Marjorie Batchelder McPharlin, who after Paul McPharlin's death in 1948 became something of a *grande dame* of American puppetry, traveled around the world learning about contemporary and historic forms of puppet theater. Invited to be part of an international jury at the 1958 International Festival of Puppet Theaters in Rumania, Batchelder was impressed with the artistic advances made by Asian

puppet theaters and the state-supported puppet companies of Communist countries. She later wrote that the shows she saw there were "a revelation of what can be done with puppets." But upon her return to the United States she was critical of the general situation of American puppet theater. "There did not seem to be much advance in the quality of American puppet theater," she wrote, adding that "I was not able to engage in the kind of puppetry here that I had come to believe was essential to make puppetry a significant branch of the performing arts."

The persistence of the first wave's goal of puppetry as art theater was also articulated by veteran puppeteer Ralph Chessé. In a 1981 interview he summed up the contemporary situation of puppetry, noting that it "has had to move with the times," and that a "change in the style of puppets," of which the Muppets were the best example, meant that scripts "had to be written to appeal to the mass audience." Nightclub puppeteers, Chessé said, "have developed clever, fast numbers often put on by a single puppeteer, and these are financially successful." However, Chessé added, "art must not be judged by degrees of financial success. The true artist does not like to make compromises." Chessé's vision of a "true artist" of puppetry hearkens back to the idealism of the Little Theater Movement years, and Chessé thought that some form of government funding—which he had experienced with the Federal Theater Project—might be a means of supporting "cultural entertainment." However, realistically speaking, Chessé felt that an uncompromisingly artistic puppet theater was not within reach. "To be financially successful," he said, "the puppeteer must go commercial."

Chessé's sense of the unlikelihood of an independent American puppet art theater was compounded by the widespread belief that puppet theater was children's theater. This was a popular point of view in the postwar years, when American puppetry was dominated by children's television shows, advertising, educational projects, and religious shows, and there did not seem to be any room for a twentieth-century puppet theater for adult audiences. In 1959 a show entitled *People and Puppets* opened in New York City, presenting what the *Puppetry Journal* called "a production for adults at a strictly adult level." The show included George Bernard Shaw's play for puppets, *Shakes vs. Shaw*; W. B. Yeats's *The Cat and the Moon*; and a reprise of Cervantes's puppet episode from *Don Quixote*, which Remo Bufano had performed to great success in Manuel de Falla's opera version thirty-four years earlier. But this

late-1950s collection of mainstream works from the early puppet art theater movement received poor critical reviews, and *The Puppetry Journal* wondered if it was in fact at all possible to present puppet theater for adults in 1959. "The P of A (Puppeeteers of America) would be delighted to learn of the establishment of an adult puppet theater," Vivian Michael wrote, "but are we ready for it?" Categorically ruling out the possibility of reaching adults with puppets, Michael nonetheless held out a slim hope for the future: "Maybe if we all strive for just a little more perfection in our work," she continued, "that 'adult recognition' will come along some day."

Despite the obstacles to creating adult-oriented puppet theater, puppeteers did not forget the idealistic goals of earlier decades. A puppeteer as commercially successful as Burr Tillstrom, for example, could still yearn to create his own puppet art theater, and puppeteers such as Basil Milovsoroff persisted in pursuing puppetry as an independent art. Nor can it be said that commercially successful puppet theater did not express important concepts about American culture, because it did, especially in the creation of popular characters that came to exemplify particular aspects of modern American character. Punch, Kasperl, Petrushka, and variety-show puppets fulfilled this function in the nineteenth century; the

modern American versions of those cultural icons happened to have names like Ollie, Kukla, and Howdy Doody.

## SIXTIES PUPPET THEATER: A NEW WAVE

The state of late-1950s puppetry would soon be affected by a new generation of puppeteers in the later decades of the twentieth century, who created a third puppet revival, matching the energy that sparked the earlier ones. On the one hand the 1960s revival would be epitomized by the inspired finesse of television and film puppetry as an artistic, educational, and entertainment medium, especially through Jim Henson's Muppets, and on the other by a return to the artistic and political roots of puppet theater as serious culture, which in the United States was initiated by Peter Schumann's Bread and Puppet Theater.

By the time Jim Henson started his career as a puppeteer, Burr Tillstrom, Frank Paris, the Roses, George Latshaw, and others had already established how effectively television puppet theater could reach a wide audience. Henson devoted his work almost entirely to that form. In 1954, at the age of eighteen, he began performing puppets on a Saturday morning program in Washington, D.C., and by the following year had his own show, *Sam and Friends*, on a local

NBC affiliate. Henson and his partner Jane Nebel (who later became his wife) built and performed soft, foam-rubber and cloth-covered hand puppets with moveable mouths and rod-controlled hands, which they named Muppets. Henson's central character and alter ego, Kermit the Frog (see p. 96), evolved as Henson and his growing band of puppeteer colleagues, including Frank Oz and Jerry Juhl, progressed through a series of network television appearances and hundreds of commercials. The Muppets reached one peak of creativity as the stars of the Children's Television Workshop show *Sesame Street*, which began broadcasting in 1969. Henson's work on *Sesame Street* showed that using puppets to educate and entertain children could become its own form of high art, full of subtlety and wit that engages adults as well as children. The Muppets' appearances on *Saturday Night Live*, and then the creation of *The Muppet Show* in 1975, showed how a puppet theater for adults could be achieved on television. It was in the medium of film that Jim Henson found some of the most creative outlets for his work, for example in the experimental object-performance short *Time Piece* or in full-length features like *The Dark Crystal*, through which he could pursue the kinds of ideas, stories, and images that challenged him. The success

of Henson's film work led to the creation of his Creature Shop studios in London and Los Angeles, which developed new puppet and animatronic techniques for scores of commercial films. However, despite all this success in developing puppetry as a mass-media form, Henson also persisted in examining and supporting the roots of puppet theater as live performance. He produced a series of documentary films on traditional puppet theater and created the Jim Henson Foundation to promote new forms of live puppet theater that pursued the kind of art puppet theater goals first articulated in the Little Theater Movement. Henson died suddenly of pneumonia in 1990, but his company, Jim Henson Productions, has continued to flourish, and thousands of puppeteers around the world look to him as an inspiration and example.

For a few months in the mid-sixties Jim Henson shared a workshop space, in the basement of a library in New York City, with a recently arrived German sculptor and choreographer in his mid-thirties named Peter Schumann. Henson had migrated to New York after his initial television work, but Schumann had come to the city after making avant-garde dance and performance in postwar Germany. While Henson's puppet work took place for the most part in television studios, where puppeteers focused on the dynamics of puppets on a video screen, Schumann made mask and puppet shows for downtown performance spaces, where performance art and postmodern dance were being invented; for Lower East Side storefronts and loft spaces, where fellow artists like Claes Oldenburg were creating Happenings; and for the streets of New York City, where his puppets became part of political demonstrations, first for community issues such as Puerto Rican tenants' rights, and then, more importantly, for the emerging movement against the Vietnam War. In a way, Schumann's interests in the artistic and political possibilities of puppet theater echoed those of Remo Bufano forty years earlier, although Schumann was able to pursue the avant-garde possibilities of puppet theater much further than Bufano had and never turned to Broadway to legitimize his work.

Schumann's Bread and Puppet Theater benefited from its director's confidence in the capacity of puppet theater to achieve the highest possible goals of modernist performance. This confidence was due to Schumann's connection to the European experience of avant-garde performance, which already had pursued puppet theater as one of the many possible "multiple streams" of modern performance. Schumann's particular sense of a modern art puppet theater also happened to include the possibility

of political content, or, perhaps more specifically, an understanding of theater as what the eighteenth-century German playwright Friedrich Schiller called a "moral institution." Bread and Puppet Theater has combined these interests in art and politics for almost thirty years in a succession of productions ranging from hand- and rod-puppet shows to giant outdoor parades and pageants using twenty to one thousand performers. In the heated cultural environment of the Vietnam War years, Schumann was able to articulate the passionate intensity of the anti-war movement in a series of indoor and outdoor puppet shows (including *Fire, A Man Says Goodbye to His Mother, The Gray Lady Cantatas, The Birdcatcher in Hell*, and *Hallelujah*) using a variety of different puppet techniques and in

This large puppet is the Queen of Spain from Bread and Puppet Theater's *Story of Masaniello*, a modern mystery play based on the life of an 18th-century revolutionary leader. The puppet, one of a pair of regal figures used in the play, is shown exhibited at the Detroit Institute of Arts in 1982.

**S**panish artist Joan Miró designed and built this large costumelike puppet for a 1978 production of the play *Mori el Merma* (*Death to the Monster*). The figure was constructed of foam rubber covered with cloth, not unlike Jim Henson's Muppets, and formed over a wicker structure, a centuries-old tradition.

street processions in New York and Washington, D.C. Bread and Puppet became well known in Europe, where its contributions to puppet modernism were immediately recognized.

In 1970 Schumann moved with his family and his company to Vermont, where the puppet troupe became well established, presenting giant outdoor spectacles. Bread and Puppet continued to support itself by touring indoor and outdoor shows (which often incorporated scores of local volunteers) across North America, Europe, and Latin America. In 1976 a cross-country tour, which included a stop at the Detroit Institute of Arts, Bread and Puppet performed *Ave Maris Stella*, a mask and puppet production set to the music, written by French composer Josquin des Prés (ca. 1440-1520), for a mass of the same name. A few years later, the company performed *Story of Masaniello* (see p. 101) a modern mystery play based on the tragic life of an eighteenth-century Neapolitan revolutionary leader, accompanied by traditional southern Italian folk music played by the group Pupi e Fresedde. Both *Masaniello* and *Ave Maris Stella* were typical Bread and Puppet productions: they earnestly espoused the performance of culturally valuable but rarely presented work—medieval and southern Italian folk music in these cases— in brilliant puppet spectacles whose story lines had definite political (or moral) resonance for contemporary audiences.

The success of Peter Schumann's work in Europe reflected the continuity of puppet modernism on that continent. Puppet theaters had been a fundamental element of socialist countries since the end of World War II, and scores of puppet theaters sprung up in Europe throughout the 1960s and '70s. A particular example can be found in the over-life-size puppets Catalan artist Joan Miró designed and built for *Mori el Merma* (*Death to the Monster*), a 1978 show performed by the Catalan theater group La Claca (Catalunya is the fiercely independent northeast region of Spain). Miró's large costumelike puppets were made of foam rubber covered with cloth and formed over woven wicker structures. This structure points to an important historical aspect of Miró's modernist puppets: the use of wicker structures is part of the centuries-old tradition of Catalan giant puppets used in street processions for religious events. Miró designed his puppets for La Claca when he was in his eighties, but in his youth he had lived the life of a modernist artist in Paris and had been fully exposed to the currents of avant-gardism that so clearly valued puppet theater. Both Miró and La Claca director and playwright Joan Baixas specifically based *Mori el Merma* on Alfred

Jarry's 1896 *Ubu Roi*. The villainous king Mori, modeled on Jarry's Ubu, was also a representation of the recently deceased Spanish dictator Francisco Franco, who had severely repressed Catalan culture during his thirty-six-year rule. La Claca's performance of a high-art, political spectacle was a test of the new democratic forces at work in post-Franco Spain, and while it reflected traditional Spanish puppet traditions as well as twentieth-century traditions of avant-garde performance, it was also an example of the cultural activism triggered by the ferment of the 1960s and '70s, the same reinvigorated sense of political puppet theater that characterized Bread and Puppet.

## THE BLOSSOMING OF LATE-CENTURY PUPPET THEATER

The work begun by Henson and Schumann in the sixties was continued in an ever-widening circle of new puppetry, which by the end of the century had created a flourishing array of different forms and styles. In Los Angeles, London, and New York puppeteers who had grown up in the company of television puppetry, like Stan Winston and Brian Henson (who headed Jim Henson Productions after his father's death in 1990) created live puppet performances and stop-action animated work for film and television, as well as increasingly

mechanized means of operating puppets for such high-grossing Hollywood movies as *Jaws*, *Jurassic Park*, the *Star Wars* epics, and *Babe*. Their use of multi-operator, live puppets in film production competed with, and sometimes complemented, the development of computer animation, which could also create spectacular non-realistic images for mass consumption, although without the physical presence of puppets and puppeteers on a film set. By the end of the century, it seemed as if computer animation would edge out puppetry as the preferred mass-media form of spectacle imagery, but in fact both these forms of performing object theater continue to thrive. The high-tech use of three-dimensional figures operated directly or indirectly by puppeteers still echoes some of the oldest forms of hand puppets and marionettes, while even higher-tech use of two-dimensional images projected on a computer screen echoes the oldest forms of shadow theater.

At the same time, a younger generation of artists, actors, and puppeteers followed Schumann's example by pursuing live puppetry as a means of making experimental theater or performance art. Some of the younger group of art puppeteers, such as Amy Trompetter, Paul Zaloom, Julie Taymor, and Sandy Spieler (of In the Heart of the Beast Puppet Theater), had direct experience

Larry Reed trained as a *dalang* (puppet master) on a trip to Indonesia. His huge shadow puppets, from the production *In Xanadu*, show the influence of the traditional shadow plays performed there. Reed's puppets are actually worn on the puppeteer's body, unlike the Indonesia shadow figures, which are a type of rod puppet. In another change, Reed has replaced the traditional oil lamps used to illuminate the puppets with 1,500-watt xenon projector bulbs, resulting in an image the size of a movie screen. Two of the puppets from *In Xanadu* will enter the McPharlin Collection in 2001.

working with Bread and Puppet Theater, while others, such as Theodora Skipitares, Janie Geiser, and Larry Reed came to puppet theater on their own. Reed and Julie Taymor in particular were influenced by their experiences in Indonesia, where they learned how shadow figures (*wayang kulit*) and other forms of mask and puppet performance were central pillars of indigenous culture. Both Reed (who trained as a *dalang* in Indonesia) and Taymor returned to the United States dedicated to the goal of making serious art theater with puppets in their own country. Taymor ultimately achieved success on Broadway with *The Lion King* and in films such as *Titus*. The San Francisco-based Reed gained critical and popular acclaim with such productions as *In Xanadu*, *The Wild Party*, and *Wayang Listrik*.

In the Midwest, the blossoming of late-century puppet theater included the 1998 creation of Saw Theater by Mark Fox and Tony Luensman in Cincinnati. Saw Theater seeks to create "cutting edge" puppet works and quite specifically focuses on live, adult art theater rather than children's entertainment. *Account Me Puppet*, a 1999 production commissioned by the Detroit Institute of Arts, was inspired by John Milton's *Paradise Lost* and uses an array of old European and Asian puppet traditions (marionettes, Bunraku, shadow) as well as new technological innovations (projected images, film, and video). In its variety of puppet techniques and its dedication to creating serious theater with puppets, the company builds on the development of American puppet theater since the

Photo by Jim Moore

1960s but also realizes many of the goals of early twentieth-century pioneers like Paul McPharlin, who would clearly have understood what Saw Theater is doing and why.

The recent turn of the century has also seen a continuing presence of puppets in political discourse. Since 1974 the midwestern company In the Heart of the Beast Puppet Theater has used annual puppet spectacles in Minneapolis to make participatory theater that deals with political issues affecting the community in which it is based. And 1999 and 2000 saw a flourishing of puppet street theater in connection with the political issues of globalization raised by meetings of the World Trade Organization in Seattle. Puppeteers around the United States, inspired in part by Bread and Puppet Theater's continuing work, routinely incorporate

giant figures and masked characters in street processions and performances. The force of such work can be gauged by the fact that, in 2000, the Philadelphia police arrested seventy puppeteers and destroyed over one hundred of their puppets to prevent them from participating in demonstrations protesting the Republican National Convention held in that city. Something about the strength of live puppet performance clearly worried the Philadelphia authorities.

## CONTEMPORARY PUPPET THEATER AND RELIGION

Just as puppets have persisted as a political presence, they have also thrived in religious performance. Bible stories, which had been central to European puppet theater long after European actors' theater

had been secularized, persisted as a kind of modern art theater in Paul McPharlin's *Noël* (see p. 67) and in the Purimspiels by Remo Bufano and Meyer Levin (see p. 62). But modern American puppetry also began to present religious stories not only for their story value but as acts of implied or outright religious devotion, especially in what came to be known as the Christian puppet movement. As early as 1936 the Martin Marionettes of Cincinnati had "reverently offered" their version of the *Passion Play*, and Nancie Cole's *Juggler of Our Lady* was performed in New York churches in 1959. A focused effort to present puppet shows on Christian themes was made by the Stevens Puppets, with their *Joan of Arc*, *Passion Play*, and *Nativity* shows from the late 1930s through the

The Detroit Institute of Arts commissioned puppeteers Mark Fox and Tony Luensman to write and perform a work specifically designed as adult art theater. *Account Me Puppet*, inspired by John Milton's *Paradise Lost*, was the result. This scene is from a 1999 exhibit "Fallen Stages: Drawings, Pages, and Chapters from *Account Me Puppet*," installed at the Detroit Institute of Arts to coincide with the authors' performance of the play. *Account Me Puppet* combines an array of European and Asian puppet traditions.

1960s (see p. 73). Peter Schumann's Bread and Puppet Theater has long used the cultural traditions of Christian performance—nativity plays, passion plays, the structure of the Catholic mass, and the wealth of western religious music, from Bach cantatas to early American "Sacred Harp" music—but for the purpose of creating contemporary theater that can address moral and political issues. The Christian puppet movement that developed in the late 1970s, on the other hand, turned to puppet theater as ministry, a means of reaching out to Christian audiences. A Fellowship of Christian Puppeteers was created in 1974 to share resources and ideas among the hundreds of American puppeteers who use puppets as part of their ministry, and Christian puppet and ventriloquism festivals have become a popular part of American religious culture. Christian puppeteers rely for the most part on Muppet-inspired rod and hand puppets, and focus not so much on the traditional Bible stories that have been the core of European religious puppet theater since medieval times, but instead on contemporary characters and situations.

## INSTITUTIONAL GROWTH

The new generation of American puppeteers at the end of the twentieth century enjoyed the support of a variety of institutions that had developed since the 1960s. Frank Ballard started a professional college-level puppetry program at the University of Connecticut in 1968, and Vincent Anthony created the Center for Puppetry Arts in Atlanta in 1977. In 1992 Cheryl Henson and Leslee Asch of the Jim Henson Foundation produced the first Henson International Festival of Puppet Theater in New York, which they have continued to present every two years. Puppeteer Janie Geiser initiated a program of puppetry studies at the California Institute of the Arts in 1999. In a way, all of these institutions echoed the efforts of Paul McPharlin and his colleagues in the 1920s and 30s; it is clear, however, that these end-of-century efforts encountered wider support and recognition because of the slow but steady progress their predecessors had achieved during the past hundred years.

## PUPPETRY AT THE TURN OF THE TWENTY-FIRST CENTURY

The American puppetry experience, although arising from Old World traditions, was quite different from that in Europe. While Europe had long fostered a tradition of the arts as the bearers of culture and ideas, American cultural history had established a tradition of the arts as primarily a means of commercial entertainment. The earliest expressions of American puppet modernism, connected to the Little Theater Movement, paralleled European modernist goals of creating a form of non-commercial, culturally rich performance, in contrast to the straightforward focus on commercial success so central to nineteenth-century puppet traditions. This ideal of an art existing apart from the demands of the marketplace helped spawn connected ideas: that puppets could be useful as modern educational and social tools, which could teach children and adults how to live better. But just as the Little Theater Movement's greatest playwright, Eugene O'Neill, was irresistibly drawn from Greenwich Village's Provincetown Playhouse uptown to Broadway, so were American puppeteers drawn by desire or necessity into the commercial possibilities of modern puppet theater, which in many cases proved to be lucrative, or at least capable of supporting a puppeteer's existence. In the second wave of puppet modernism, during and after the Depression, the idea of art theater generally faded further into the background, but in the 1960s a burst of new interest in the possibilities of puppetry emerged in the work of Jim Henson and Peter Schumann.

The succession of puppet renaissances during the twentieth century says something about the resilience of the old art of puppet theater in the constantly changing, increasingly technologically oriented environment of modern life. The fact that the periodic rebirths were necessary means that puppet theater has never fully established a fixed role for itself in contemporary American society, and this, in a way seems fitting. Puppet theater has always been a quirky, mysterious, often subversive, and sometimes peripheral art form, and the fact that it has had to constantly reinvent itself in order to survive is probably a good thing. Its capacity for survival will be a primary resource for its work in the twenty-first century. ◆

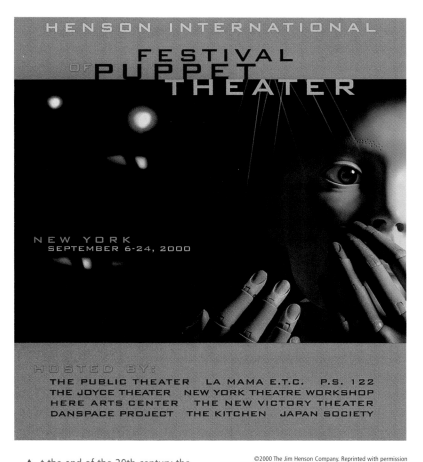

At the end of the 20th century the biennial Henson International Festival of Puppet Theater provides a showcase for modern puppetry performances. For the 2000 event (above), the festival featured performances by twenty-six puppet companies from fourteen countries.

# APPENDIX

## PUPPETS AND TOYS

One of the strengths of the McPharlin Collection is its array of toy puppets, which come in a variety of forms. In some cases, they are smaller and more cheaply made versions of popular puppets from a particular country or region, often items to be taken home by tourists. In other cases, toy puppets constitute their own particular form of children's entertainment.

The toy theaters or "Juvenile Dramas" invented in England at the end of the eighteenth century were mass-produced proscenium-arch stages, sets, and characters representing popular live theater entertainments of the day. These sets were assembled, colored and decorated, and plays were performed, using an accompanying truncated script, by middle-class English children for the next two centuries. By following the popular stage hits of the day, English toy theaters featured a stream of melodramas and pantomimes—the same repertoire also performed by nineteenth-century marionette troupes. The popularity of toy theaters spread all across Europe and into the United States. Later variations on the form included Punch and Judy theaters and miniature versions of popular puppet shows, such as a tin stage and lead figures for a German Kasperl show. The German Kasperl characters, not unlike those of a Punch show, were also reproduced as hand puppets, with cast papier-maché heads and colorful floral print bodies, allowing children to perform their own

This type of toy theater was first mass-produced in England at the end of the 18th century. For the following two centuries, middle-class English children assembled, colored, and decorated the stages and created their own productions.

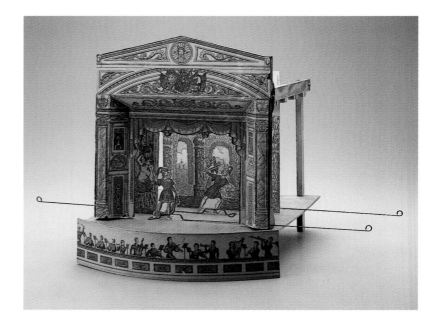

versions of the popular puppet theater at home. Similar child-sized versions were made of Sicilian, Czech, and Mexican marionettes.

As the twentieth century progressed, puppeteers and manufacturers realized the educational and recreational function of children's puppets and more were mass-produced as toys. In the 1930s Cleveland puppeteer Helen Haiman Joseph designed a toy version of the "Mr. Clown" marionette she used in her own shows; the toy version was then produced by Cleveland's Playfellow Shops. In 1935 Joseph and the Playfellow Shops created a challenging, colorful do-it-yourself marionette construction kit—the first such kit manufactured in the United States. Joseph's kit featured all the basic materials for building marionettes, including six heads, wooden pieces to be made into limbs and torsos, cloth for making costumes, control bars, and paints, and even puppet scripts. Around the same time, the American Crayon Company mass-produced its own toy marionettes, based on the clowns and minstrel figures of traditional nineteenth-century entertainments (see p. 110). "Hazelle's Marionettes" were also produced, offering "Realistic-Educational-Entertaining-Nonbreakable" puppets ready to perform. Concurrently in England Waldo Lanchester, whose puppet troupe performed traditional marionette variety shows, designed a marionette kit for mass distribution.

Manufactured by Jonda Puppetcraft Studios, Lanchester's marionette kit featured the basic parts of a marionette figure, made of a silvery material called "Leetex."

By the 1950s and 1960s the popularity of marionettes had been superseded by hand puppets. Burr Tillstrom had helped market toy animal hand puppets by including them in the shows he performed at the Marshall Field's department store in the 1950s. Similar puppets were manufactured in the 1960s in

Commercially manufactured toy puppets reflected popular traditions. These two mass-produced papier-mâché German hand puppets are commercial versions of characters from that country's Kasperl tradition.

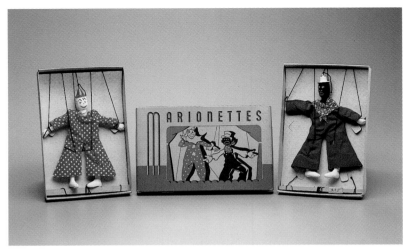

In the 1930s, the American Crayon Company mass-produced toy marionettes, based on the popular puppet variety shows of the 19th century. The same racial stereotyping found in the older theatrical entertainment was carried over to children's puppets, as the minstrel figure in this set shows.

communist Czechoslovakia. In the same decade a soft, cloth-bodied hand puppet kit was manufactured by a company in Palo Alto, California, showing the influence of new Muppet-style puppet construction. Although these post-World War II forms all offered the possibility of stimulating entertainment for children, they also show the extent to which toy puppets had come to differ from the earlier originals upon which they were ostensibly based. In place of the exaggerated, often grotesque, and potentially malevolent demeanor of traditional hand puppets, these children's versions feature benign, almost blank expressions and a minimum of strong character traits, a measure of how twentieth-century puppet theater was considered to be improved

and made safe for children by smoothing over or eliminating its acerbic and contrary tendencies.

The connection between toys and puppets is basic and essential: the deep importance of toys as indispensable elements of childhood is related to the strength of puppets as a theater form for all ages. In the twentieth century educators and puppeteers realized that the creation and use of puppets was a basic skill of value for all children. The challenge of manipulating objects has, since the 1980s, often shifted focus to the projected images on computer screens— a technological evolution of the earlier forms of manipulation represented in the McPharlin Collection. ◆

## SUGGESTIONS FOR FURTHER READING

## COLLECTION DATA

Baird, Bil. *The Art of the Puppet.* New York: Bonanza, 1973.

Barreiro, Juan José and Marcela Guijosa. *Titeres Mexicanos: memoria y retrato de automatas, fantoches y otros artistas ambulantes.* Mexico City: Roche, 1997.

Batchelder, Marjorie. *Rod Puppets and the Human Theater.* Columbus, Ohio: Ohio State University, 1947.

Bell, John, ed. *Puppets, Masks, and Performing Objects.* Cambridge, Mass.: MIT Press, 2001.

Blumenthal, Eileen and Julie Taymor. *Playing with Fire: Theater, Opera, Film.* New York: Abrams, 1995.

Brecht, Stefan. *Peter Schumann's Bread and Puppet Theatre.* New York: Routledge, 1988.

Brown, Foreman. *Small Wonder: The Story of the Yale Puppeteers and the Turnabout Theatre.* Metuchen, N.J.: Scarecrow Press, 1980.

Bufano, Remo. *The Show Book of Remo Bufano.* New York: Macmillan, 1929.

Crothers, J. Frances. *The Puppeteers Library Guide: A Bibliographic Index to the Literature of the World Puppet Theatre.* Metuchen, N.J.: Scarecrow Press, 1971.

Joseph, Helen Haiman. *Book of Marionettes.* New York: B. W. Huebsch, 1920.

Efimova, Nina. *Adventures of a Russian Puppet Theatre.* Translated by Elena Micoff. Birmingham, Mich: Puppetry Imprints, 1935.

Hunt, Tamara Robin. *Tony Sarg: Puppeteer in America, 1915-1942.* North Vancouver, B.C.: Charlemagne Press, 1988.

Jurkowski, Henryk. *A History of European Puppetry,* 2 vols. New York: Edwin Mellen Press, 1996.

Lano, David. *A Wandering Showman, I.* East Lansing, Mich.: Michigan State University Press, 1957.

Lomatuway'ma, Michael. *Children of Cottonwood: Piety and Ceremonialism in Hopi Indian Puppetry.* Lincoln, Nebr.: University of Nebraska Press, 1987.

Magon, Jero. *Staging the Puppet Show.* Miami: Miami Press, 1976.

Marsh, Benjamin. *Chinese Shadow-figure Plays and Their Making.* Detroit, 1938.

McCormick, John and Bernie Pratasik. *Popular Puppet Theatre in America: A History, 1524-1948.* Cambridge: Cambridge University Press, 1998.

McPharlin, Paul and Marjorie Batchelder McPharlin. *The Puppet Theatre in America: A History, 1524 to 1948,* with a supplement: *Puppets in America Since 1948.* Boston: Publishers Plays, 1969.

McPharlin, Paul ed. *A Repertory of Marionette Plays.* New York: Viking Press, 1929.

Speaight, George. *The History of the English Puppet Theatre.* London: George G. Harrap & Co., 1955.

Stalberg, Roberta. *China's Puppets.* San Francisco: China Books, 1984.

Tillis, Steve. *Toward an Aesthetics of the Puppet: Puppetry as a Theatrical Art.* New York: Greenwood Press, 1992.

Wright, Richardson. *Hawkers and Walkers In Early America: Strolling Peddlers, Preachers, Lawyers, Doctors, Players, and Others, from the Beginning to the Civil War.* Philadelphia: J.B. Lippincott, 1927.

### Cover

*Juggling Clown*, 1883/1919, Walter E. Deaves (American, 1854–1919); wood, cloth, and paint, height 73.7 cm (29 in.). Founders Society Purchase, Paul McPharlin Memorial Fund (54.123).

### Contents Page

*Punch and Judy Set*, mid-1800s, American; wood, cloth, and paint, height of Punch: 54.6 cm (21$^1/_2$ in.). Gift of Lettie Connell (59.341.1–12).

### Chapter 1

*Self-Portrait*, 1936, Paul McPharlin (American, 1903–1948); plastic, wood, paint, and cloth, height 62.9 cm (24$^1/_2$ in.). Gift of Mr. and Mrs. W. H. J. McPharlin and Marjorie Batchelder McPharlin (52.368)

*Mask*, 19th/20th century, Dan culture, Ivory Coast; wood, feathers, height 21.6 cm (8$^1/_2$ in.).

Hand puppet: *Devil*, 20th century, Bross Puppets (German, established 1900); wood, cloth, and paint, height 55.9 cm (22 in.) Founders Society Purchase, Paul McPharlin Memorial Fund (74.102). Bunraku puppet: see ch. 3 (X1989.2540); Rod puppet: *Ygraine*, see ch. 4 (52.392); Marionette: *Private Eye*, see ch. 5 (1987.46); Over-life-size: *Billy the Kid* puppets, George Latshaw (American, born 1923); (X1989.3877); Shadow puppet: Javanese *wayang kulit* (X1989.2384).

### Chapter 2

*Man, Woman,* and *Capitano*, 18th century, Venetian; wood, plaster, cloth, glass, and paint, height of Capitano: 57.2 cm (22$^1/_2$ in.). Gift of Helen Reisdorf in memory of her brother Jack L. Reisdorf (52.152, 52.154, 52.153). *Stage*, Venetian, 18th century; wood and paint. Gift of Mr. and Mrs. Cedric Head (55.206).

*Fancy Gentleman*, Italian, possibly Venetian, 18th century; painted wood and cloth, height 71.8 cm (28$^1/_2$ in.). Gift of Donald Oenslager (55.234).

*Venetian Gentleman*, late 19th century, Pietro Radillo, (Italian, 1820–95). Founders Society Purchase, Paul McPharlin Memorial Fund (59.395, 59.396).

*Orlando Furioso: Woman, Priest,* and *Knight in Armor*, late 19th century, Sicilian; wood, metal, and paint; height of Priest: 48.3 cm (19 in.). (X1989.1264, 73.177, 73.110).

*Grand Turk*, 19th century, English; painted wood and cloth, height 61 cm (24 in.). Founders Society Purchase, Paul McPharlin Memorial Fund (61.210).

*Juggler, Tightrope Walker*, and *Clown*, 19th century, English; cloth and carved and painted wood, height of juggler: 40.6 cm (16 in.), height of clown: 45.7 cm. (18 in.). Founders Society Purcahse, Paul McPharlin Memorial Fund (61.205, 61.213, 61.204).

*Guignol Hand Puppet Set*, French, late 19th century; painted wood, cloth, and leather, height of Guignol: 55.9 cm (22 in.). Top row: Gift of Mr. and Mrs. W. H. J. McPharlin and Marjorie Batchelder McPharlin (52.344, 53.345, 53.348). Bottom row: Founders Society Purchase, Paul McPharlin Memorial Fund (57.251, 57.250, 57.252).

*Punch and Judy Hand Puppet Set*, late 19th century, George "Punch" Irving (American); wood, glass, cloth, leather, and fur, height of Punch: 64.8 cm (25$^1/_2$ in.). Gift of Mr. and Mrs. W. H. J. McPharlin and Marjorie Batcheler McPharlin (52.322–52.336).

*Punch*, detail, 1882/1898, Daniel Meader (American, 1856-1929); wood, cloth, paint, and glass, height 113 cm (44$^1/_2$ in.). Founders Society Purchase, Paul McPharlin Memorial Fund (54.142).

*Devils*, 1882/1898, Daniel Meader; wood, paint, and gauze foil. Founders Society Purchase, Paul McPharlin Memorial Fund (54.157, 54.158).

*Grand Turk*, 1882/1898, Daniel Meader; wood, paint, cotton, lace, and felt, height 149.9 cm (59 in.). Founders Society Purchase, Paul McPharlin Memorial Fund (54.160).

*Opera Singer/Hot Air Balloon*, 1882/1898, Daniel Meader; wood, cloth, and paint, height 113 cm (44$^1/_2$ in.). Founders Society Purchase, Paul McPharlin Memorial Fund (54.162).

*Chinaman*, 1882/1898, Daniel Meader; wood, paint, metal, and cloth, height 61 cm (24 in.). Founders Society Purchase, Paul McPharlin Memorial Fund (54.156).

*Old Biddy* and *Paddy*, 1882/1898, Daniel Meader; wood, cloth, leather, and paint, heights 91.4 cm (36 in.). Founders Society Purchase, Paul McPharlin Memorial Fund (54.141, 54.140).

*Harlequin*, 1882/1898, Daniel Meader; wood, paint, sequins, lace, and gold ribbon, height 95.3 cm (37½ in.). Founders Society Purchase, Paul McPharlin Memorial Fund (54.143).

*Scaramouche*, 1882/1898, Daniel Meader; height 97.8 cm (38½ in.). Founders Society Purchase, Paul McPharlin Memorial Fund (54.137).

*Skeleton*, 1883/1919, Walter E. Deaves (American, 1854-1919); wood and paint, height 63.8 cm (25½ in.). Founders Society Purchase, Paul McPharlin Memorial Fund (54.128).

*Diver* and *Octopus*, 1903, Walter E. Deaves; wood, paint, leather, and cloth, height of Diver: 72.4 cm (28½ in.). Founders Society Purchase, Paul McPharlin Memorial Fund (54.122, 54.130).

*Male and Female Box Puppets*, early 20th century, John Lewis (American); painted wood, cloth, buttons, and beads, height of man: 45.1 cm (17½ in.). Gift of the Goodwill Indsutries of Detroit (54.542, 54.543).

*Chinese Dancer* and *Trick Clown*, early 20th century, John Lewis; plaster, wood, paint, and cloth, height of clown: 74.9 cm (29½ in). Gifts of the Goodwill Industries of Detroit (54.535, 54.539).

*Greek Soldier*, ca. 1935, Harry Tsouleas (American, born Greece, active first half of 20th century); fiber board, height 41.3 cm (16½ in.). Gift of Mr. and Mrs. W. H. J. McPharlin and Marjorie Batchelder McPharlin (52.588).

*Chinese Ball Juggler*, late 19th century, Lano Family (American); papier-mâché, wood, and silk, height 52.4 cm (20⅝ in.). Gift of Mr. and Mrs. W. H. J. McPharlin and Marjorie Batchelder McPharlin (52.407).

*Elephant Trainer*, ca. 1910, Jesse Jewell (American, 1878–1941); wood, cloth, and paint, height 78.7 cm (31 in.). Founders Society Purchase, Paul McPharlin Memorial Fund (66.190).

*Circus Performers*, late 19th/early 20th century, Rosete Aranda Puppet Troupe (Mexican); plaster, wood, paint, cloth, and leather, height of Strongman: 33 cm (13 in.). Gift of Mr. and Mrs. W. H. J. McPharlin and Marjorie Batchelder McPharlin (52.469, 52.472, 52.475, 58.467).

*Don Folías*, 20th century, Rosete Aranda Puppet Troupe; plaster, wood, paint, cloth, and plastic, height 44.5 cm (17½ in.). Gift of Mr. and Mrs. W. H. J. McPharlin and Marjorie Batchelder McPharlin (52.470).

## Chapter 3

*Demon*, Indian; shadow puppet (X1989.3887).

*Barbarian General* and *Frog Demon*, Chinese; shadow puppets (X1989.3998, X1989.4321).

*"Painted Face" Marionette*, Chinese (X1989.1253).

*Te-Yung on a Bicycle*, 20th century, Chinese; height 29.9 cm (11½ in.). Gift of Mr. and Mrs. W. H. J. McPharlin and Marjorie Batchelder McPharlin (52.527).

*Beautiful Lady* and *Samurai Bunraku Puppets*, 20th century, Japanese; wood with brocaded costumes, height of Samurai: 127 cm (50 in.). Gift of Marjorie Batchelder McPharlin (X1989.2540, 52.400).

*Kathpulti Marionettes*, 20th century, Indian. Gift of Mr. and Mrs. Cedric Head in memory of Mabel Kingsland Head (56.65), (X1989.2226). Founders Society Purchase, Paul McPharlin Memorial Fund (56.35). Gift of Mr. and Mrs. Cedric Head in memory of Mabel Kingsland Head (56.64).

*Tolu Bommalata Shadow Figure*, Indian; height 129.5 cm (51 in.). (X1989.3888).

*Pår Painting*, Indian; gouche on canvas, 121.9 x 548.6 cm (4 x 18 ft.). (X1989.2523).

Javanese puppets: *wayang kulit* shadow puppet, leather and traces of gold (X1989.2259); *wayang kletek* rod puppet, wood (X1989.2254); *wayang golek* rod puppet, early 19th century; wood. Founders Society Purcahse, Paul McPharlin Memorial Fund (74.103).

*Nang Talung Shadow Puppets*, 19th century, Thai. Founders Society Purchase, Paul McPharlin Memorial Fund (58.366.L-N).

*Karagöz and Haçivat in a Boat*, Turkish (X1989.560).

*Karagöz* and *Watchman*, Turkish (X1989.559, X1989.558).

## Chapter 4

*Algovale*, *Ygraine*, and *Tintagiles*, 1937, Marjorie Batchelder (American, 1903–97); wood, cloth, and paint, height of Algovale: 65.4 cm (25½ in.). Gifts of the artist (52.394, 52.392, 52.391).

*Queen* and *Dancer*, ca. 1914, Michael Carmichael Carr (American, active 1907–28); papier-mâché, height of Queen: 45.7 cm (18 in.), height of Dancer: 48.9 cm (19½ in.). Gifts of Helen Haiman Joseph (58.9, 58.10).

*Peasant Woman* and *Petruska*, 1937, Russian; papier-mâché, paint, and cloth, height 50.8 cm (20 in.). Gifts of Catherine Reighard (62.259, 62.258).

*Robin Hood*, 20th century, Tony Sarg (American, 1880-1942); carved wood, paint, cloth, and leather, height 69.9 cm (27½ in.). (X1989.2850).

*The Other King*, 20th century, Remo Bufano (American, 1894–1948); papier-mâché, cloth, steel, ermine, and paint, height 73 cm (28½ in.). Founders Society Purchase, Paul McPharlin Memorial Fund (59.351).

*Ahasuerus*, *Esther*, and *Mordecai*, 20th century, Remo Bufano; papier-mâché, wood, paint, cloth, metal, and leather, height of Mordecai: 57.2 cm (22½ in). Founders Society Purchase, Paul McPharlin Memorial Fund (59.364, 59.366, 59.365).

*Walrus* and *Carpenter*, 1932, Remo Bufano; wood, cloth, paint, and plaster. Gift of the Museum for the Arts of Decoration of the Cooper Union (54.325, 54.326).

*Messenger*, *Shepherd*, and *Blinded Oedipus*, 1931, Remo Bufano; papier-mâché and cloth, height of Shepherd: 307.3 cm (121 in.). Gift of Cedric and Lee Head in memory of Mabel Kingsland Head (54.506, 54.506, 54.508).

*Bishop*, ca. 1925, Helen Haiman Joseph (American); cloth, wood, paint, gold ribbon, jewels, and lace, height 54 cm (24½ in.). Gift of the artist (58.16).

*Ada Forman*, 1921, Lilian Owen Thompson (American, 1879–1958); papier-mâché, nylon, cloth, paint, silk, and jewels, height 74.3 cm (29½ in.). Gift of Mr. and Mrs. W. H. J. McPharlin and Marjorie Batchelder McPharlin (52.426).

*Ghost of the Future, Bob Cratchit*, and *Scrooge*, early 20th century, Lilian Owen Thompson; Ghost: cellophane, cloth, and nylon netting, Bob Cratchit and Scrooge: papier-mâché, cloth, leather, glass, paint, wire, and rope, height of Ghost: 94 cm (37 in.). Gift of Mr. and Mrs. W. H. J. McPharlin and Marjorie Batchelder McPharlin (52.429, 52.427, 52.428).

*Drum Dance: Male Figure, Hsia Ying-Chun in Dance Costume*, and *Spirit*, 1929, Paul McPharlin (American, 1903–48). Gift of Mr. and Mrs. W. H. J. McPharlin and Marjorie Batchelder McPharlin (52.509, 52.506, 52.515).

*Camel Procession*, 1929, Paul McPharlin; cardboard and wood, height 40.6 cm (16 in.). Gift of Mr. and Mrs. W. H. J. McPharlin and Marjorie Batchelder McPharlin (52.522).

*Three Kings*, 1929, Paul McPharlin; plastic wood, cloth, and paint, height of Indian King: 52.1 cm (20½ in.). Gift of Mr. and Mrs. W. H. J. McPharlin and Marjorie Batchelder McPharlin (52.381).

*The Angel Gabriel*, 1929, Paul McPharlin; plastic wood, cloth, paint and feathers, height 49.5 cm (19½ in.). Gift of Mr. and Mrs. W. H. J. McPharlin and Marjorie Batchelder McPharlin (52.378).

*Mozart and Pupil*, 1930/32, Paul McPharlin; plastic wood, cloth, and paint, height of Mozart 61 cm (24 in.). Gift of Mr. and Mrs. W. H. J. McPharlin and Marjorie Batchelder McPharlin (52.452, 52.451).

*Pianist and Singer of the 1890s*, 1930, Paul McPharlin; plastic wood, cloth, and paint, height of Singer 61 cm (24 in.). Gift of Mr. and Mrs. W. H. J. McPharlin and Marjorie Batchelder McPharlin (52.455–.456).

*Ringmaster*, 1936, Paul McPharlin; wood, plastic wood, cloth, and paint, height 64.8 cm (25¹/₂ in.). Gift of Mr. and Mrs. W. H. J. McPharlin and Marjorie Batchelder McPharlin (52.351).

*Chinaman*, 1936, Paul McPharlin; plastic wood, paint, and cloth, height 54.6 cm (21¹/₂ in.). Gift of Mr. and Mrs. W. H. J. McPharlin and Marjorie Batchelder McPharlin (52.353).

*Krazy Kat* and *Joe Stork*, 1930, Paul McPharlin; Krazy Kat: plastic wood, cloth, and paint, Joe Stork: plastic wood, cotton, feathers, and paint, height of Joe Stork: 62.9 cm (24³/₄ in.). Gift of Mr. and Mrs. W. H. J. McPharlin and Marjorie Batchelder McPharlin (52.447–.448).

*La Hire* and *Joan of Arc*, 1946, Martin T. Stevens (American, 1904-1983) and Olga Stevens (American); height of La Hire: 63.5 cm (25 in.). Gift of the artists (55.187, 55.188).

*Cleopatra*, 1946, Martin T. and Olga Stevens; height 52.1 cm (20¹/₂ in.) Gift of the artists (55.185).

*Roman Soldier* and *Christus*, 1946, Martin T. and Olga Stevens. Gift of the artists (55.189, 55.188).

*Jack and the Beanstalk*: *Mother, Cow, Jack*, and *Giant*, ca. 1940, Romaine and Ellen Proctor (American); height of Giant: 77.5 cm (30¹/₂ in.). (X1989.1248).

*Tinker, Priest, Girl*, and *Two Novices*, 1930, Perry Dilley (American, 1896–1963) plastic wood, paint, and cloth, height of Tinker and Priest: 55.9 cm (22 in.). Gift of the artist (54.316–.320).

*Oberon*, 1924, Perry Dilley; wood, cloth, and padded wire, height 61.9 cm (24³/₈ in.). Gift of Mr. and Mrs. W. H. J. McPharlin and Marjorie Batchelder McPharlin (52.417).

*Emperor Jones*, detail, 1928, Ralph Chessé (American, 1900–91); wood, cloth, paint, and leather, height 63.5 cm (25 in.). Founders Society Purchase, Paul McPharlin Memorial Fund (69.66).

*Lem, Emperor Jones* and *Armchair, Smithers*, and *Formless Fear*, 1928, Ralph Chessé; wood, paint, cloth, and leather, height of Lem: 58.4 cm (23 in.). Founders Society Purchase, Paul McPharlin Memorial Fund (69.70, 69.66, 69.80, 69.68, 69.77).

**Chapter 5**

*Greta Garbo on Roller Skates*, 1939, Lauer Sisters (American); plastic wood, cloth, and paint, height 63.5 cm (25 in.). Gift of the artists (X1989.2018).

*Spanish Dancers*, mid-20th century, Lauer Sisters (American); plastic wood, cloth, and paint, height of male dancer: 66 cm (26 in.). Founders Society Purchase, Paul McPharlin Memorial Fund (X1989.1242–.1243).

*Self-Portraits*, mid-20th century, Lauer Sisters; papier-mâché, height of tallest: 61 cm (24 in.). (X1989.1241.1–.3).

*Josephine Baker*, 1937, Frank Paris (American, 1914–84); wood, paint, cloth, sequins, and jewels, height 88.9 cm (35 in.). Gift of the artist (55.470).

*Sonja Henie*, 1937, Frank Paris; wood, paint, cloth, feather, and jewels, height 97.8 cm (38¹/₂ in.). Gift of the artist (55.469).

*GE Man*, 20th century, Burr Tillstrom (American, 1917–85); height 291.5 cm (114¹/₂ in.). (X1989.3377).

*Franklin D. Roosevelt as Punch's Baby*, 1925/50, Alfred Wallace (American, 1914–85); plastic wood, stuffing, felt, cotton, and paint, height 57.5 cm (22⁵/₈ in.). Gift of Mr. and Mrs. W. H. J. McPharlin and Marjorie Batchelder McPharlin (52.361).

*The Tired World*, 1950, Alfred Wallace; plastic, wood, iron rod, and paint, height 66 cm (26 in.). Gift of the artist (56.7).

*John L. Lewis*, 1950, Alfred Wallace; plastic, wood, cloth, and paint, height 61 cm (24 in.). Gift of the artist (56.12).

*Charles de Gaulle*, 1950, Alfred Wallace; plastic wood, cloth, and paint, height 56.5 cm (22¹/₂ in.). Gift of the artist (56.8).

*Land of Oz Marionettes: Guardian, Tip, Pumpkin Head, Mombi*, and *Tin Woodsman*, ca. 1950, Burr Tillstrom; height of Mombi 47.6 cm (18¹/₂ in.). Gift of the Burr Tillstrom Copyright Trust, Richard W. Tillstrom, Trustee (X1989.2794, X1989.2791, X1989.2785, 2000.104, X1989.2792).

*Pied Piper* and *Rat*, 1961, George Latshaw (American, born 1923); Gift of the artist. (62.263, 62.264).

*Private Eye*, 1935, Margo Rose (American 1903–97) and Rufus Rose (American, 1904–75); wood and fabric, height 63.5 cm (25 in.). Founders Society Purchase, Paul McPharlin Memorial Fund (1987.46).

*Self-Portrait*, 1964, Jero Magon (American, 1900–1995); plastic wood, cloth, and paint, height 47 cm (18¹/₂ in.). Gift of the artist (1983.48).

*Bug*, 1930/40, Basil Milovsoroff (American, 1906–92); wood paint, metal, and plastic, height 15.9 cm (6¹/₂ in). Gift of Herb Scheffel (54.314).

*Kermit the Frog*, 1969, Jim Henson (American, 1937–90); cloth, foam rubber, metal rods, and plastic, height 33.7 cm (13¹/₂ in.). Gift of the artist (71.383).

*Dance Costume*, 1976-77, Joan Miró (Spanish, 1893-1983); stuffed, painted costume, height 142.2 cm (56 in.). Gift of Harold and Maureen Zarember in honor of Michael Kan (1991.1014).

**Appendix**

*Pollack's Original Victorian Theater* (X1989.526).

*Man and Devil*, 1900/1950, German; hand puppets. Gift of Mr. and Mrs. W. H. J. McPharlin and Marjorie Batchelder McPharlin (52.375, 52.373).

*Two Clown Marionettes*, ca. 1935, American Crayon Company (1925-1945). Gift of Mr. and Mrs. W. H. J. McPharlin and Marjorie Batchelder McPharlin (52.487, 52.488).

**Back Cover**

*Dancer*, see ch. 4 (58.10); *Punch*, see ch. 2 (52.322); *Tolu Bommalata Shadow Figure*, Indian. (X1989.3889)

# INDEX

**ABOUT THE AUTHOR**

John Bell is a puppeteer, teacher,
and historian. He is a member of
Great Small Works theater company
and an Assistant Professor of
Performing Arts at Emerson College,
Boston. His work in puppetry began
with Bread and Puppet Theater, with
which he has worked since the
mid-1970s.

**PHOTO CREDITS**

Unless otherwise noted, all
photographs © The Detroit
Institute of Arts. Photography
by Dirk Bakker with additional
photography by Robert Hensleigh.

Cover photo by Robert Hensleigh.

Archival photographs and playbills
on pages 8, 9, 27, 40, 59, 69, 72,
and 76, from the Paul McPharlin
Puppetry Collection.

Page 107—Cover figure *Pupil*
courtesy of Elizabeth King;
cover photograph by Eric Beggs.

**REFERENCES FOR QUOTATIONS**

Page 15—Charles Magnin, quoted in
Majorie H. Batchelder, *Rod-Puppets
and the Human Theater* (Columbus:
Ohio State University, 1947), xiii.

Page 19—Anatole France, quoted
in Harold B. Segel, *Pinocchio's
Progeny: Puppets, Marionettes,
Automations, and Robots in
Modernist and Avant-Garde
Drama* (1995), 80.

Page 98—George Bernard Shaw,
quoted in Segel, *Pinocchio's
Progeny*, 1-2.

Page 100—Peter Schuman, quoted
in *The Oxford Illustrated History of
Theatre* (Oxford: Oxford University
Press, 1995), 528.

**BACK COVER**

*From left to right:*
Strings: *Dancer*, Michael Carmichael
Carr, marrionette (see p. 55).

Hands: *Punch*, George Irving, hand
puppet (see p. 22).

Shadows: *Tolu Bommalata Shadow
Figure*, Indian. (X1989.3889).